Teleworking
Thirteen Journeys to the Future of Work

Andrew Bibby is a writer and journalist who has made a particular study of the development of teleworking. He is the author of a practical teleworking handbook *Home is Where the Office is*, and a regular contributor to *The Observer*, the *Independent* and other national newspapers and magazines.

Front cover photographs: aerial view of London; rural Ireland (Stuart Brown Photography)

Teleworking
Thirteen Journeys to the Future of Work
Andrew Bibby

Calouste Gulbenkian Foundation, London 1995

Published by Calouste Gulbenkian Foundation
98 Portland Place
London W1N 4ET
Tel: 0171 636 5313

© 1995 Calouste Gulbenkian Foundation

The right of Andrew Bibby to be identified as the author of this work has been asserted in accordance with the Copyright, Designs and Patents Act 1988.

ISBN 0 903319 74 8

British Library Cataloguing-in-Publication Data
A catalogue record of this book is available from the British Library

Designed by Maddison Graphics 0171 380 0336
Printed in England by Whitstable Litho 01227 262311
Distributed by Turnaround Distribution Ltd 0171 609 7836

Acknowledgements

I met great interest and cooperation whilst researching this book, and am grateful to many people for their assistance.

I particularly acknowledge the support and help of Alan Denbigh of the Telecottage Association, and would also like to thank the following: Jane Berry and Simon Berry, Warwickshire Rural Enterprise Network; Imogen Bertin, Cork Teleworking Centre; Margaret Birkett, BT; Tim Blaxter, Crossaig Ltd; Dominic Bourton, Kington Connected Community; John Bryden, Arkleton Trust; Liz Burn and Amanda Stewart-Richardson, Strathdon Telematic Services; Anthony Capstick, Instant Search; Stuart Carruthers, TAGish; Dave Carter, Manchester City Council; Nic Carter-Jones, CEB Telecentre; Brian Cogan, Forfás; John Coleman-Smith; Ian Culpin, DG XIII, European Commission; Ian Dempsey, Bangladesh House EVH; Manuela Finetti, ISPO, European Commission; Andrew Gillespie, University of Newcastle upon Tyne; Stephen Graham, University of Newcastle upon Tyne; Mike Gray and Nick Good, BT; Roy Guthrie, Guthrie Creative Services; Janet Harvey, North Tyne Telecottage; David Henderson and Stuart Robertson, Highlands and Islands Enterprise; Colin Hensley, ISPO, European Commission; Gary Herman; Mike Holderness; Norman Howard, BT Community Affairs; Vande Hutchings; Ursula Huws; Peter Johnston, DG XIII, European Commission; Amelia Jones, Bronllys and Talgarth Telecentre; Graham Knight, Moira Replan; Debra Lee and Jim McCurrach, Grampian Regional Council; Graham Lightfoot and Nana Luke, East Clare Telecottage; Drew Llewellyn, Boon telecottage; John Lyons, Cigna; Sheila McCaffrey and Michael McCaffrey, KITE telecottage; Cathal McCarthy, Global-Res International Ltd; Alison McKechanie; Horace Mitchell, Management Technology Associates; Paddy Moindrot, Telecottages Wales; Joyce Morgan, Powys County Council; Les Morgan, Hoskyns; Janet Nuth, Codford Telecottage; Gerard O'Neill, Henley Centre Ireland; Jak Radice and Andy Robinson, Chorlton Workshop EVH; Rosemary Rattney; Ranald Richardson, University of Newcastle upon Tyne; Neil Sandford, Menter Powys; Julia Seal, Mere Telecottage; Claire Shearman; David Souter; Dave Spooner, Labour Telematics Centre; Bill Walsh, MSF; Sue Wilding, Community Enterprise Project, Presteigne; and the staff of Manchester Business School Library, the UMIST Library, the British Library Business Information Service, the City Business Library. A personal acknowledgement, too, to Jane Scullion for her help and encouragement.

Contents

Introduction *1*

1 **Whalley, Lancashire**
  The telework business: who is teleworking? *6*

2 **St Michaels on Wyre, Lancashire**
  The experience of being a home teleworker *12*

3 **Southampton**
  Why BT is sending workers home; corporate teleworking programmes *20*

4 **Blairgowrie and Helensburgh**
  Crossaig Ltd: the telework company *28*

5 **Forres**
  Outsourcing in the Highlands *38*

6 **Cork**
  Call centres for the European market *48*

7 **Cyberspace** *57*

8 **Kinawley, Co Fermanagh**
  Developing a telecottage *63*

9 **Talgarth, Powys**
  The telecottage movement in Britain and Ireland *71*

10 **Manchester**
   The urban context *79*

11 **Maiden Newton, Dorset**
   What future for the telecottages? *86*

12 **Brussels**
   The European Commission and telework *97*

13 **Strathdon, Aberdeenshire**
   Plans for a teleworking future *108*

Conclusion *111*

Bibliography *119*

Abbreviations

ACD	Automated call distribution
BPO	Business process outsourcing
CAD	Computer aided design
CTC	(Scotland) Community Teleservice Centre
DTI	(UK) Department of Trade and Industry
DTP	Desk-top Publishing
ERDF	(EU) European Regional Development Fund
ESF	(EU) European Social Fund
EVH	Electronic village hall
ICT	Information and computer technologies
IDA	(Ireland) Industrial Development Agency
ISDN	Integrated Services Digital Network
IT	Information technology
MSF	(UK) Manufacturing, Science and Finance trade union
OCR	Optical character reader/recognition
PC	Personal computer
SME	Small and medium-sized enterprise
STAR	(EU) Special Telecommunications Action for Regional Development

Introduction

This is a book about opportunities and dangers. It explores the ways in which the experience of work may change in the future, and indeed has already begun to change. It considers the new working practices which are being made possible by information and telecommunications technologies as they increasingly coalesce. In particular, it is about the phenomenon which has become known as 'teleworking'.

We are moving, it is said, into the information age. Industrial mechanisation required large numbers of people to work and live closely together. Office workers, too, were tied to the place where the paperwork they needed for their work was processed and stored. But information held on a computer database, by contrast, can be accessed from anywhere. Using computer power and communications links we can work from wherever we choose – we can telework.

The idea of the teleworker harnessing the power of a worldwide network of information has already been a popular subject for the media. It has become linked particularly to the idea of making the home once again the workplace.

A few years ago British Telecom ran a series of national newspaper advertisements illustrated by a photograph of a delightful stone-built detached country house, complete with creepers round the porch and a rose bush in the garden. The caption read 'Office, sweet office'. The copy said, "Now, instead of you always going to the office, the office can come to you. All you need is a phone socket, a desk that overlooks the garden and the right equipment" – together, of course, with the BT products which the advert was promoting.

This is a powerful fantasy, especially for city-dwellers feeling worn down by urban pressures and dreaming the good dream of a quieter, more holistic life in the country. Telework seems to offer a modern way in which this old longing can actually be realised, without opting out of the conventional world of work altogether. Why stay in the cities when you can undertake your work just as well from a cottage in Cumbria, a croft in Caithness or – let's not rule out any of the possibilities – a chateau in Champagne? After all, if the work involves any form of information processing, then certainly in theory it can now be undertaken from anywhere.

One of the first writers to realise the possibilities which technological change was opening up was an American academic Jack Nilles, who put forward the concept of 'telecommuting' as an alternative to conventional commuting to work at a time in the early Seventies when the oil crisis had just given the American economy a deeply unwelcome shock. Another writer, Alvin Toffler, popularised the idea of electronic home-working in his 1980 book *The Third Wave* (the first wave in his version being the development of agriculture, the second industrialisation). In a book which at the time attracted considerable attention, Toffler came up with the concept of the 'electronic cottage', the home-base from which both men and women would be able to reintegrate the world of work back with the rest of their lives.

The idea of doing a day's work as a high-tech worker in a rural home, complete perhaps with BT rose bushes and creepers, is such an appealing one that perhaps I should apologise in advance for the fact that this book will not be a celebratory romp through the subject. But too much emphasis on the rural home-working scenario is preventing proper analysis of some of the other things that are taking place, which can also be defined as forms of teleworking.

Before we go any further, therefore, we need to discuss just how we should define the term. Teleworking in this book means *making use of information and communication technologies* to practise some form of *remote working*.

This is a wider definition than that used by some people. Early accounts on telework tended to focus on what could be called the 'classic' scenario, of the employee who remained on the company's payroll whilst changing from working at the employer's premises to working at home. However, this approach has increasingly been seen to be altogether too restrictive. In the first place, moves towards teleworking have also been associated with other forms of business restructuring, including an increasing use of outsourcing. In other words the number of home-based teleworkers who remain direct employees of their parent firm is more than matched by the number of freelance teleworkers operating as independent self-employed sub-contractors and consultants.

In addition, whilst home-based telework is certainly happening, it is overshadowed in terms of overall economic importance by other developing forms of teleworking practice. Too much stress on the home as the base for teleworking can exclude consideration of, for example, the rapid growth in the number of community-based telecentres and telecottages. The establishment of what can now clearly be described as a telecottage movement in Britain and Ireland is important, and something I will be exploring later.

However, in terms of its economic and employment implications, a much more significant development in recent years has been the use made by companies of satellite or remote offices. As we shall see, these are typically modern units on out-of-town industrial estates where back-office information processing work or telephone enquiry and sales work is being relocated, away from companies' corporate headquarters. The working situation of staff in these centres may be far removed from the rural work-at-home teleworker image, but nevertheless still constitutes a form of teleworking.

My broader definition of teleworking to include developments like this is now generally the one followed by other writers. The 1993 *Teleworking Study* for the Department of Trade and Industry, for example, interpreted telework to mean "all forms of location independent work, including working from home, working in local telecentres or telecottages, [and] work by executives and others away from their normal office base."[1] Another recent report from a group of academic researchers adopted a similar position: "We take the view … that the focus of investigation should be the diffusion and impact of new information and communications technology on the spatial organisation of work."[2]

Since the first writings of Jack Nilles and Alvin Toffler the published literature on teleworking has grown to enormous proportions – academic research, government reports, conference proceedings, European Commission documents, mass-market handbooks, journalistic musings. Among all this, there is much that is interesting and useful, but there's also much hype and hot air. We already have a potential information overload. So where among all the other books on the subject should this one be filed? What are my particular aims?

This work was commissioned by the Calouste Gulbenkian Foundation with a clear, practical objective: to investigate what is actually happening on the ground, underneath all the telerhetoric. Although my central focus is on developments in Britain and Ireland, I try to put these in an international context. Europe is suffering the strains of unemployment, so the questions are urgent. How can the technology create new work opportunities? Where is the new work coming from and what will it feel like when (– if? –) it comes?

The journeys of the book's title are in one sense simply a writer's device. But I did travel extensively during the winter of 1994 and the first half of 1995 as part of my research, and I was intrigued, surprised and stimulated by some of the things I found going on. My theme expanded as my research took shape, so that this book is not simply a series of studies of particular teleworking ventures. It is an exploration of what is happening to work today.

During the journeys which follow, I ask some questions.
- What sort of work is being created?
- How do these developments relate to current business restructuring and changing styles of management?
- What is the role of public bodies and the community in this process of change?

- What are individuals gaining or losing (both financially and in other ways) from this work? Or, put another way: what about the workers?

I begin with the familiar scenario of the individual teleworker, and then move on to consider the use being made by companies of remote satellite offices and call centres. Later in the book I turn from the commercial to the community scene, to explore how a wide range of voluntary organisations are attempting to develop work opportunities through teleworking. Finally, after an examination of the role of the European Commission in the promotion of telework, I return to the teleworkers themselves, to end with a series of conclusions based on my findings.

Through all the pages which follow, I try to remember one thing: telework is not a technological issue, but a social issue. The future is not determined by technology, but created by humans.

References

1 Department of Trade and Industry *Teleworking Study* 1992-1993. Final report by Horace Mitchell, Eric Trodd, Brameur Ltd, September 1993.
2 *Review of Telework in Britain: Implications for Public Policy*. Prepared for the Parliamentary Office of Science and Technology by Andrew Gillespie, Ranald Richardson and James Cornford, Centre for Urban and Regional Development Studies, University of Newcastle upon Tyne, February 1995.

Journey 1
Whalley, Lancashire
The telework business: who is teleworking?

Whalley is as good a place as any to start. In mediaeval times, the town had status: the monks of Whalley Abbey played a dominant role in the economic life of this part of central Lancashire, and the Cistercian foundation itself owned land for miles around. But fortunes change with the years. Now Whalley is just another pleasant small English town, and the Abbey is a pile of picturesque ruins in the riverside meadows.

I'd come to Whalley to meet Anthony Capstick and to find out about his business, Instant Search. Anthony had left London and a job at the *Financial Times* in 1991 to return to the area of Lancashire where he'd grown up. The decision to set up his own business was, perhaps, a risky one: nevertheless four years on Instant Search is growing nicely, turnover up last year to about £160,000, prospects encouraging.

Anthony describes Instant Search as a business information bureau. In fact, the service he offers is a very simple one. Customers ring through to ask for information on companies – the names of the directors, perhaps, or the last reported profit figures – and the details required are faxed back in response a few minutes later. Summary information on a British limited company costs £14. A more comprehensive search on creditworthiness may cost £30. You pay immediately and automatically, by credit card.

Instant Search is a business of our time. Anthony Capstick has created it by using the opportunity opened up by technological development over the past few years, and in particular by the growing convergence of computer and telecommunications technologies – what tends now to be described as 'information and communication technologies' or ICT.

There are three necessary tools he needs for the business to work: the ordinary telephone, for customers' initial calls, and the fax machine, to deliver the answers, are two of these.

The heart of the business, however, is the ability to link up ordinary PCs to distant computers over the standard public telephone network. Instant Search's PCs are attached to modems, which in turn are plugged into telephone sockets. This means that, instantaneously, Anthony Capstick can delve into the main Companies House database or go to one of the commercial on-line database providers such as Infocheck, regardless of where these computers physically happen to be located. When necessary he is able just as easily to scour a database in mainland Europe, the USA or elsewhere in the world. Once on-line, national barriers vanish.

Instant Search does not itself compile the information it sells. Indeed, the main databases used are readily available for anyone with the time to do their own searching. This sort of D-I-Y research is cheaper: a Companies House search, for example, normally costs only a few pounds if you undertake it yourself. But Anthony Capstick says that his business's selling point is not the information itself but the method and speed of its delivery. He draws an analogy with the newspaper industry, and describes himself as an electronic newsagent rather than a publisher. And he makes a more general point: information by itself has little value, it's what's done with the information that counts.

Instant Search has now developed to the stage where four full-time workers have been employed, with two other part-time jobs also dependent on the business.

But where is Whalley's place in all this? The answer is clear: although Instant Search is physically based in Whalley (in a converted semi in a quiet side-street opposite an old-fashioned dress shop, to be precise) the technology effectively renders its geographical location irrelevant. For the purposes of a business like this, Whalley can be anywhere. Whalley is Wimbledon, is Winchester, is Wick. Or – increasingly – Whalley could be Wroclaw, or Witswatersrand, or West Bengal.

"I'm here in Whalley because I'm from this area, and I like it,"[1] Anthony Capstick says. He decided to take the plunge into business after five years at the *Financial Times*, during which time he found himself increasingly advising other journalists on how to use modems to file copy electronically whilst abroad. He and his wife Katie already had a house in the area, and their first child had arrived. The *FT* seemed unconvinced at his suggestion that he could successfully work for them from the Ribble Valley. But a short time previously Companies House had launched its new on-line search facility, and Anthony felt that there was a potential business here to be exploited. Instant Search began initially from a base in the main bedroom at home.

Retold like this, it sounds like the sort of story which newspapers (including the *Financial Times* itself) have been running at regular intervals over recent years. The idea of moving from urban stress to rural peace is a powerful dream for many of us.

Combine this with talk of high technology and information superhighways, and it's not surprising that these stories are so attractive both to journalists and their readers.

But it is once we go beyond the individual stories to try to generalise about teleworking that we can begin to encounter some problems. How many people are doing it? What sort of work are they doing? Where are they living?

There is certainly a problem with the numbers. All sorts of figures have been bandied about in recent years. The authors of BT's 1993 handbook *Teleworking Explained*[2], for example, claimed to have demonstrated that there were 5.89 million teleworkers in the USA and 1.27 million in Britain. However, despite the exactness of the figures given, the authors freely admitted that they had been forced to rely on a number of assumptions, extrapolations and estimations. They also included mobile workers and employed staff working for a minority of their time from home offices, as well as home-based teleworkers.

An attempt at a more rigorous statistical survey has recently been carried out by the German based analysts Empirica, as part of the European Commission funded TELDET project.

"According to the results of the surveys in 1994 the penetration of telework in European organisations is around five per cent and the actual number of teleworkers in the five largest EC countries approximately 1.1 million. The UK and France are the countries with the highest telework penetration in organisations, with around seven per cent of the organisations practising telework,"

Empirica reported to the Telework 94 conference held in Berlin.[3] The UK had about 560,000 teleworkers, Empirica claimed. However, this figure falls to about 130,000 when only 100 per cent home-based teleworkers are considered.

One difficulty, of course, is that not everyone teleworks full-time. Many companies have informal arrangements whereby staff can take work home on an occasional basis. Horace Mitchell, of the consultancy firm Management Technology Associates, has distinguished between 'marginal' telecommuters (one or two days a month), 'substantive' telecommuters (one or more days a week) and 'dominant' telecommuters (three or more days a week).[4]

Another point is that not all home-based workers necessarily qualify for the teleworker tag. The 1991 Census produced a figure of 1.2 million people in Great Britain who could be defined as working mainly at home, or living at their place of work. This is about five per cent of the working population.[5] But the problem from our point of view is that this figure includes, for example, many farmers and agricultural workers, people 'living over the shop' and workers such as caretakers and hotel staff who are resident in their workplaces. It is not possible from the Census data to separate out the specific subsection of this group who could be said to be teleworking.

We are on slightly firmer ground with the 1992 teleworking survey undertaken by Ursula Huws for the Department of Employment, which contacted over 1,000 employers. Ursula Huws found that 113 firms were employing some people who spent at least half their working time at home and of these 58 met the survey's definition of teleworking (this involved using both computers and telecoms links to undertake work remotely). The actual occupations of these 58 firms' teleworkers were surprisingly diverse: the largest occupational groups by percentage were consultancy (10 per cent), secretarial/administration (10 per cent), computer professionals (6 per cent), training/education (6 per cent), data entry/typing (6 per cent), research (5 per cent) and sales/marketing (5 per cent).

Ursula Huws concluded:

> "Our calculations suggest that, although one employer in ten is employing some form of home-based worker, and one in twenty at least one teleworker, these home-based workers make up somewhat less than one percent of the total workforce, of whom only a half (less than one worker in 200) is a genuine teleworker."[6]

However, the survey specifically excluded any analysis of employees working from remote locations other than their homes. Neither, perhaps more significantly, did it cover the freelance sector. In other words, self-employed teleworkers, or those running very small companies, are not reported in the findings.

I intend to take a broader definition of telework than simply the traditional focus on the employer-sponsored home-based worker. I believe that this definition will help to widen the debate on teleworking away from overly narrow parameters. However, it also means that meaningful discussion on the number of people teleworking becomes even more difficult.

What the various surveys do offer, however, is a warning against hype: media enthusiasm about telework is not necessarily reflected in the number of people actually experiencing it for themselves. "It is clear that home-based teleworking remains a marginal form of work in the UK," say the academics from the University of Newcastle upon Tyne in their 1995 *Review of Telework in Britain*.[7]

It is also clear that the familiar telework image associated with BT's delightful country cottage may also be misleading. Whilst information and communications technologies enable the geographical location of the workplace to become irrelevant, this does not mean that everyone who is teleworking has already packed their bags and moved.

In fact, we should perhaps be picturing our typical teleworker as living not in a rural retreat but in a conventional house in the suburbs. "Electronic homeworking is predominantly an urban and suburban phenomenon and is likely to remain so," say the Newcastle researchers. "These results give no support to any argument that teleworking is most likely to be found in rural areas. On the contrary, it seems more likely to be found where population density and land values are high," says Ursula Huws in her Department of Employment report.

The point is worth bearing in mind. Clearly, the whole population of these islands cannot suddenly relocate itself away from the urban areas: Wimbledon would simply be unable to decamp en masse to Whalley, for example. Whatever possibilities technology may permit, the development of teleworking will not lead to an overnight radical transformation of how we live and work.

References

1 Except where otherwise indicated in these notes, all direct speech quotations in this book are from interviews conducted by the author during research (Spring 1995), and subsequently checked back with each interviewee prior to publication.
2 *Teleworking Explained* by Mike Gray, Noel Hodson and Gil Gordon, John Wiley and Sons, 1993.
3 'Telework in Europe: penetration, potential and practice (Has it lived up to expectations?)' by Werner B Korte, Norbert Kordey, Simon Robinson (empirica GmbH) in *Telework 94, New Ways to Work: Proceedings of the European Assembly on Teleworking and New Ways of Working*, Berlin 1994.
4 *Plenty of Work, Not Many Jobs?* Horace Mitchell (Management Technology Associates), Version 1, January 1995.
5 See: 'Working at home: estimates from the 1991 Census' by Alan Felstead and Nick Jewson in *Employment Gazette*, March 1995.
6 *Teleworking in Britain*. A report to the Employment Department by Ursula Huws, Analytica, Employment Department, research series no 18, October 1993.
7 *Review of Telework in Britain: Implications for Public Policy*. Prepared for the Parliamentary Office of Science and Technology by Andrew Gillespie, Ranald Richardson and James Cornford, Centre for Urban and Regional Development Studies, University of Newcastle upon Tyne, February 1995.

Journey 2

St Michaels on Wyre, Lancashire

The experience of being a home teleworker

It is a pleasant journey west from Whalley, skirting the edge of Longbridge Fell and the Forest of Bowland. I wanted to combine my journey to Lancashire with a visit to St Michaels on Wyre, a few miles inland from the coast, to meet Alison McKechanie and John Coleman-Smith, two long-standing members of the OwnBase group.

Alison runs her counselling business from a self-contained suite of rooms at her home there. John, an engineer by background, took retirement a few years ago and now undertakes management training and conference organisation from his home in Cheshire. He'd arranged to drive up the M6 that day to meet me.

OwnBase is about as grass-roots as organisations come. It describes itself as a network, linking people who find themselves working from home.

> "Members can exchange skills, ideas and solutions covering both work and personal related topics", says one of its publicity leaflets. "This provides the opportunity for members to learn from other homeworkers' experiences, make new contacts or simply let off steam".

The printout of the jobs which OwnBase members between them undertake shows a good number of computer consultants and programmers, and several translators, technical authors, indexers and publishers. But the group at the moment also includes, for example, a sign maker, a jeweller, a calligrapher, a poet and a potter. This means that not all of OwnBase's 200-odd members would necessarily meet a strict definition of teleworking. But whatever technology they may or may not use, OwnBase members clearly share many of the same experiences.

There can be great satisfaction and enjoyment in working from home. But there can be pressures, too. One OwnBase member, an IT consultant, describes how it felt to be starting work from home:

> "For the last two years while launching my business, I have had to learn to work in my home environment. At home, my two twin girls work full-time at eating, sleeping and playing. My wife, nanny and cleaner come and go, and I am expected to be Mr Professional Consultant on the telephone while desperately trying to ignore the instinct to check on my screaming children three doors away. It takes an almost super-human tenacity to stay at my home-office desk … "[1]

It was feelings very similar to these which led Chris Oliver, a former social worker, to set up OwnBase in the summer of 1986. Although she is not directly involved today, in many ways the organisation continues to reflect her personality.

Chris Oliver has described how she made the transition from working for a national organisation (which "provided status, salary and a never-faltering stream of work") to life as a freelance in a rural part of Wales. Looking back on the occasion of OwnBase's third birthday, she explained:

> "By New Year 1986, I had ground to a halt on a long-term, solitary, self-motivated (and funded) project. Realising I was starved for the nourishment of like-minded company, I typed up a simple newsletter, photocopied it, and circulated it to some 100 home-based people, suggesting that we could do with a regular point of contact. Knowing that there was nothing abnormal about my feeling of deprivation, I reminded those other homeworkers what they told me about the effects of 'creeping isolation'."[2]

OwnBase took off after Chris Oliver's embryonic organisation was featured in a *Guardian* article in July 1986 and 50 readers quickly signed up. Alison McKechanie recalls how she was one of those early members: "I sent Chris a photograph of me and my cat in my office. She replied, sending me a photo of the view from her window."

Chris's interest in each new member and her personal touch were strong elements in the early years of the group, and were reflected in the newsletters produced which tended to be informal and chatty in tone (John Coleman-Smith admits looking back that some people found it all "a little cottage and chintzy"). Nevertheless, OwnBase grew steadily in numbers, helped with some seedcorn grant funding. OwnBase reached a peak membership of about 380 and spawned a number of active local groups.

Alison McKechanie herself was active in a local group in the small town of Garstang, north of Preston. "Everybody did different things, but we'd meet to discuss who was a good accountant, for example, or where to get letterheads done," she says.

OwnBase's history suggests that groups like these tend to peter out after a time. As Alison says, either people move back into conventional paid employment "or they're doing so well that they haven't got time to socialise".

The national organisation, too, has found that new members join, stay for a time, but then fail to renew their annual subscriptions. To some extent this means that the newsletter – the main forum for communication – tends to go over the same issues again and again. On the other hand, people who find themselves newly working from home need access to the basic information, and may want to share the same experiences as others who have been in the same situation before them.

OwnBase has carefully eked out the initial £10,000 grant funding it received, and still has a few thousand pounds in the bank. However, with membership currently standing at about half the level it once reached, the organisation's committee members clearly are aware that there is a question mark over the future of the group. "Like a lot of small organisations, there is no back-up for a re-launch and nobody doing the PR," Alison says.

As OwnBase has demonstrated, sharing the pleasures and problems of working from home can be preferable to trying to cope alone. Any attempt at collective self-help by home-based workers, however, has to overcome the problem that the potential constituency is geographically isolated in individual homes up and down the country. Perhaps, too, the experience of OwnBase suggests that homeworkers need something more on offer in hard business terms if they are to be persuaded to continue to renew their membership.

Some of the early enthusiasm for OwnBase transferred across to the Telecottage Association, which developed during the early 1990s and which now has a membership of about 2,400, a mixture of telecottage workers, individual teleworkers and others with a professional interest in the issue. Its bi-monthly magazine, *Teleworker*, is a lively and professionally produced publication. (I look at the work of the Telecottage Association in more detail later.)

Since 1992 there has also been another organisation, the National Association of Teleworkers, claiming to represent the interests of teleworkers. This Association (established with the support of Cable and Wireless and the Worshipful Company of Information Technologists) offers a members' newsletter and compiles an annual register of members wishing to advertise their services. The National Association of Teleworkers also engages in consultancy work for companies contemplating telework programmes.

The individuals I met whilst researching this book who were engaged in home-based teleworking were, in general, enthusiastic about their experiences. Indeed, there was sometimes in their comments an element of slight proselytising, and an understandable pride in being pioneers in new ways of living and working.

But it is important to point out that the individual's experience of telework and how they weigh up the advantages and disadvantages of their situation depends to a large extent on the work they are doing and the work status they already have. A highly-paid teleworking professional in a high-status job or a self-employed freelance developing their own business is in a very different situation to a low-status member of staff undertaking repetitive work such as data entry or telephone enquiries.

Apart from all other considerations, a well-paid professional is more likely to be able to afford a large enough house with space to spare for a separate home-office, in more attractive surroundings.

There is also a history to homeworking which pre-dates the idea of telework, and which mustn't be forgotten. The National Group on Homeworking issued a report in 1994 on the traditional world of home-based labour, normally undertaken by women and comprising such work as machine sewing, packing and routine clerical work. The NGH reported that the typical homeworker of this type worked a 36 hour week in exchange for an hourly wage of £1.28. Very few workers received standard employment rights, such as sickness and maternity pay, or had their health adequately protected.[3]

Home sweatshops may seem a long way from the gleaming technological image of the Information Age but nevertheless sewing machines and knitting machines were new technology once, not so long ago. Can we automatically assume that the teleworking experience will be very different?

The potential benefits for the individual teleworker have been mulled over by many writers on the subject.[4] These include greater work flexibility – the opportunity to manage potential conflicts between work and family demands more easily, for example. There are the obvious savings both in the time and money spent in conventional commuting to work. There is the opportunity to live where you choose, rather than where your employer happens to be based (added to this, teleworkers whose partners are relocated to other areas do not necessarily have to sacrifice their own careers in the move).

Work motivation can be greater, and the extra autonomy which teleworking entails can be fulfilling (though it can also be daunting). Teleworkers, particularly those in remote areas, can also gain access to a wider range of employment opportunities by being able to work for a wider pool of employers.

"Some see teleworking as an opportunity to bridge the 'career gap' or improve employment opportunities ... Teleworking is often not seen as [a] permanent way of life, but rather as a temporary solution to a particular set of problems," add the University of Newcastle upon Tyne researchers in their *Review of Telework in Britain*.[5]

There is also the possibility of combining work with child care. My journey to the KITE telecottage at Kinawley (chapter 8) will provide an appropriate opportunity to examine the issues of teleworking and child care in more detail; but for now it is enough to say that the idea that children can be looked after at the same time as an adult is attempting to telework from home has been rejected by almost everybody writing on the subject. What teleworking can offer for parents, however, is a more flexible working day: the opportunity to fit work around school hours, for example, or take time off to attend a school assembly. This is an important gain.

What about the possible disadvantages? Home-based workers potentially have to resolve two types of difficulty. There are, firstly, the technicalities to sort out. There are issues of workspace and equipment to consider. There is the need to ensure that household contents insurance is extended to protect work-related items, since most standard policies do not include this cover. There is a possible problem if planning permission for partial change of use is necessary (usually, it is not). In certain circumstances uniform business rates may also become payable.

Health and safety legislation applies, technically speaking, to all people at work, even those who are self-employed and working by themselves at home. There may be a further legal requirement to register under the Data Protection Act.

As we shall see, home-based workers who are undertaking outsourced work for clients may run the risk of dispute with the Inland Revenue as to whether the work is being undertaken in an employee or self-employed relationship. And of course, for the home-based self-employed as for all small businesses there are issues of marketing, book-keeping and accounting which need attention.

But if these are the technicalities, there are also the personal and emotional aspects of working from home. As Chris Oliver knew, home-based work can be an isolating experience: the feeling of being cut off from the real world of work, of missing the company of colleagues or the social interaction of a normal workplace.

There is the need to find ways to combine work-life and home-life, a process which may involve having to redefine relationships with partners and children. There is the requirement to develop the necessary self-discipline to get down to the work, to find from within the work motivation which in a conventional workplace usually is provided externally. And there are longer-term questions, too, relating among other things to career development and work status.

These sort of issues may manifest themselves in particular problems which need resolving: how to stop friends from calling round during the day for lengthy chats, how to prevent the dog barking at the wrong moments, how to discourage children from crashing the PC whilst playing computer games out-of-hours.

To what extent the benefits of teleworking outweigh these disadvantages clearly depends on the particular circumstances of each individual teleworker. As I suggest, people undertaking low-status repetitive work may have a very different experience to higher-paid professional teleworkers.

There is clearly also a gender issue here. Any discussion of home-based teleworking has to begin with the recognition that for many women the home is the place where domestic housework takes place, a form of work which is unpaid and accorded much less status in our society than the 'real' work which takes place in the external workplace. Power and money are to be found in this external world, not in the home.

As the authors of *Telework: Towards the Elusive Office* put it:

"According to the prevailing stereotype, going out to work is experienced as a 'masculine' activity, while staying at home is seen as 'feminine'. This gives the act of going out to work, or not going out, quite a different meaning for men than for women … For a man, going out to work confirms him in his role as breadwinner and provider and reinforces the separateness of the public world of his work from the private domestic sphere. Working at home, on the other hand, brings these two worlds into close proximity and confuses their boundaries …

For a woman homeworker, the problem is ... not how to break out of her traditional role as the stay-at-home, but how to survive within it, with the added stress of her paid work."[6]

References

1 'Experiences of Working from Home', Andrew Kristoffy, *OwnBase* magazine, vol 6, no 4, September/October 1994.
2 Articles in *OwnBase* magazine, vol 3, no 1, January 1991; and vol 1, no 5, 1989.
3 *Home Truths, key results from a national survey of homeworkers (National Group on Homeworking, report no 2)* by Ursula Huws, 1994.
4 My own exploration of these issues is given at more length in my *Home is Where the Office is: A Practical Handbook for Teleworking from Home*, Hodder Headline, 1991.
5 *Review of Telework in Britain: Implications for Public Policy*. Prepared for the Parliamentary Office of Science and Technology by Andrew Gillespie, Ranald Richardson and James Cornford, Centre for Urban and Regional Development Studies, University of Newcastle upon Tyne, February 1995.
6 *Telework: Towards the Elusive Office* by Ursula Huws, Werner B Korte and Simon Robinson, John Wiley and Sons, 1990.

Journey 3

Southampton

Why BT is sending workers home; corporate teleworking programmes

Margaret Birkett met me in her office, a large upstairs room of a BT block near the harbour area of Southampton. The office was surprisingly quiet for a working Friday, and near Margaret's own desk were several banks of unoccupied desks. But I should have expected this: this was the reason why I'd come.

Until the second week of January 1995, the office had been the workplace of Margaret's team of 25 sales staff, working for BT's Volume Business Sales division and handling enquiries from business customers ringing in on the 152 enquiry number. Now her team was split: 13 people were still office-based, while the remaining 12 were participating in a BT pilot scheme during which they were teleworking from home.

Yes, said Margaret, they did feel a little like pioneers. Although the Southampton teleworking project was initially set to run for a limited period of six months, the plan was – if all went well – to extend it indefinitely, and then to roll out the idea to other Volume Business Sales call centres elsewhere in the country. And, yes, Margaret assured me, so far everything was going very well.

Later that day, Margaret would take me out to one of the suburban areas north of Southampton, to let me meet one of the team members who'd joined the teleworking scheme. Vande Hutchings was upbeat, too. "This is my third week teleworking, and I feel as though I'm on holiday," she said. "Personally, I'm far more relaxed than I was in the office." She sat at her BT-supplied desk in a small spare bedroom and prepared to take the next sales enquiry, automatically routed to her via BT's

Automated Call Distribution technology. A specially installed Integrated Services Digital Network (ISDN) line meant that she had immediate access to BT's main customer databases, enabling her to call up the details she needed of each customer's account and previous sales record on the PC monitor on the desk in front of her.

For Vande, in fact, teleworking does not quite mean working from home. Instead, she has arranged to work each day from the house of a friend. As her friend also supplies stabling for Vande's three horses, this means that Vande can combine work with pleasure. "I'm now able to go riding every day in the mornings, before starting work at 1pm," she says.

Behind what seemed a wonderfully simple way of arranging the work process lay a lot of detailed planning, however. Margaret Birkett worked full-time on the pilot project for seven months, looking at both the technical and personnel implications of using home-based staff. BT's team of telework researchers and consultants, based at its research laboratory at Martlesham Heath near Ipswich, were also involved. Mike Gray, who heads the Martlesham telework team, arranged for Margaret to attend the Telecommute 94 conference held in San Francisco.

Nearer the launch date, there were other things to arrange. A BT safety manager visited all the houses where the teleworkers planned to work, to make sure they were suitable as workplaces and to check the power supply, wiring and lighting arrangements. "We emphasised the importance of health and safety. The house was to become an office environment," Margaret Birkett says. A trainer was seconded full-time to the project to run a series of preparatory training sessions for the teleworkers, including a briefing on how to operate PCs running on Windows.

All the Southampton teleworkers were existing BT employees, and all were volunteers. Joining the scheme was not automatic, however, and each person was invited to make a formal bid to join. Margaret Birkett says that she turned down some applicants. There were three criteria which would-be teleworkers had to meet. Firstly, the home had to be suitable as a workplace, free from distractions and free also from the noise of dogs. A second criterion was location: not all parts of the country currently are within telephone exchange areas where ISDN lines can be installed – and ISDN lines were essential for the scheme to work.

But Margaret also says she took into consideration people's past performance at work. "Some people I didn't encourage to apply. If they didn't perform well here, how were they going to be able to perform well at home?" she asks.

The process of selecting the Southampton teleworkers was not quite as straightforward as this may suggest, however. Initially, BT had planned to have 20 people teleworking. A few weeks before the start, however, only seven people had been recruited to take part. In the end, as we have seen, 12 joined the scheme.

Given that working from home seems such an attractive idea, why were volunteers initially so hard to find? The reason is to do with BT's own reasons for wanting to use teleworking staff. This wasn't, after all, something organised just as an employee perk. There were business reasons why teleworking was considered a good strategy.

Operating a call centre system like BT's 152 service, which is open for calls from 8am-6pm Mondays to Saturdays, requires careful rostering in order to make sure that staff are available at all times, but particularly to ensure that peak periods for calls are adequately covered. Several BT Business Volume Sales call centres are operated together – so that when Southampton is busy, for example, calls are redirected automatically to another office elsewhere.

Using teleworkers provides a welcome element of flexibility for the employer when arranging work schedules. Before the teleworking scheme started, most of the Southampton office-based staff were full-time, working 37 hours a week on a flexitime basis. Initially BT wanted to reduce the hours worked by teleworkers to 25 hours a week. Eventually – when it had become clear that it was going to be difficult to recruit enough people – the hours on offer were increased to 30. However, teleworkers are now given set hours to work, including for the first time compulsory Saturday work. Their set shifts also include the difficult hours immediately after 8am and before 6pm, before and after many flexitime staff are in their offices. "For the teleworkers, there is the positive advantage of working from home to set against the disadvantages of the set hours and the part-time hours," says Margaret Birkett. "The business reason for introducing teleworking is to manage our resources better."

Clearly, her task of supervising twelve staff who are working several miles away in their homes, rather than a few feet away across the office, raises interesting issues of management. Technology eliminates one possible difficulty: a monitor on Margaret's desk shows her exactly what calls each of her staff – home-based and office-based alike – are engaged in at any one time. This means that, should she so wish, she can check exactly which of her teleworkers is currently taking calls and who has, for example, taken a short break.

As with any sales operation there is also continual monitoring of staff performance, with incentives for those who meet sales targets. Margaret's teleworkers have been set higher performance targets than their office-based colleagues. This is partly because they are unable to take their share of the general office-based administrative tasks but it is also a recognition that working from home, away from the distractions and socialising atmosphere of the office, means that more work gets done.

The teleworkers are given a daily briefing (by E-mail or phone) of the previous day's team sales performance and achievement, and where they stand in performance terms in relation to their colleagues. Videophone links are not currently used, but may be installed later. However, there are also arrangements for face-to-face meetings. The teleworkers attend their old office once a month for review meetings and Margaret has also tried to keep both parts of her team together by arranging social events after hours. Shortly before we met, after the telework project had been running a few weeks, she had arranged a skittles evening (out of work time) for her staff. Interestingly, one initial problem which she had to sort out arose after the remaining office-based workers claimed that the teleworkers were receiving special treatment in relation to clerical support.

I'd asked Vande Hutchings whether she felt working away from the office meant that she would miss out on new job opportunities, and perhaps the chance of promotion. She replied candidly that the job gave little scope for promotion but that anyway she felt no great urge to leap up career ladders. "I've got to the stage where my children are now growing up, and I'd like to take advantage of my life as it is now," she'd said. Of the 12 Southampton teleworkers, ten are women.

I was also interested to know whether Margaret Birkett herself, who had had the opportunity to consider both the theory and practice of teleworking, was tempted to telework. She replied carefully that it wouldn't work for her personally. For her, she made clear, the development of her management career was important – and teleworking was not the best way of guaranteeing this, she implied. "It's important to keep one's profile up," she'd said. (Indeed only a few weeks after we'd met, she was promoted to a new post in Cardiff.)

It seems appropriate to focus initially in a book on telework on the Southampton pilot because it represents an excellent example of the 'classic' type of teleworking, as foreseen and described in the early literature. In fact, Southampton is not BT's first venture in this area, since for a year in 1992-3 eleven directory enquiry operators from BT's Inverness office worked at home. As at Southampton, these staff remained employees of the company.

The Inverness experiment, which was set up and monitored by the Martlesham Heath team partly as a research exercise, has been the subject of a later BT video and report:

> "Service levels were enhanced through greater flexibility, resilience and skills retention. The operators were more flexible about the hours they worked and were much more willing to work overtime and swap shifts. This flexibility allowed variations in demand to be met more easily. A more resilient service was offered through teleworkers being able to work at times when Centre-based operators could not, eg during bad weather ... A great deal was learnt from the experiment about the appropriateness and effectiveness of facilities and technologies for teleworkers ..."[1]

However, despite promoting the Inverness experiment as a success, BT has chosen not to continue the use of teleworking for its directory enquiry staff. BT argues that Inverness was never intended as a permanent arrangement. However, the considerable general cutbacks in staffing levels for the Directory Assistance service which have recently been taking place must be a factor in this decision.

More generally, BT has chosen to market the idea of telework strongly, taking national advertising to promote a series of popular booklets on the subject. (Clearly, as a telecoms company, BT has considerable interest in working arrangements which make greater use of telecoms technology.) BT's telework team at Martlesham Heath, which is now about ten-strong, also offers its expertise on a consultancy basis to other companies considering teleworking, and has produced the book *Teleworking Explained* and a series of shorter publications on aspects of telework.[2]

We saw in the last chapter that teleworking can have both benefits and snags for the individual. What about the employer's perspective? The general gist of BT's publications – and of the many other writers who have considered the advantages and disadvantages of home-based teleworkers – is that, notwithstanding the initial costs of developing pilot programmes, the employer can benefit substantially.

According to a 1990 report from the International Labour Office:

> "There is widespread consensus that large productivity gains result from telework. These are attributed to the lack of interruptions and improved concentration; increased motivation and job satisfaction; higher dedication and morale; and a higher energy level on the job due to the elimination of the wasted time and frustration of commuting."[3]

The ILO went on to quote productivity gains in US telework experiments, including an average of 43 per cent for New York Telephone, 12 per cent to 20 per cent at Control Data Corporation, 30 per cent to 40 per cent at US West and 40 per cent to 50 per cent at the University of Wisconsin Hospital and Clinics.

In Britain, the survey undertaken by Ursula Huws for the Department of Employment[4] also found evidence of gains in productivity. In a survey of 74 organisations using teleworkers, about 47 per cent believed that staff who were teleworking showed greater productivity; only five per cent thought their productivity was lower. Ursula Huws' survey also found that at least one in four companies felt that they were gaining through greater employee reliability and quality of work and through reduced rates of absenteeism and staff turnover.

Other writers have stressed the potential cost savings for companies in reduced office costs.

The Newcastle upon Tyne researchers in their *Review of Telework in Britain*[5] summarise the advantages in the following table:

Advantages as perceived by employer:
- reduced costs
- flexibility (particularly in periods of fluctuating demand)
- managing redundancies
- retain skilled staff
- recruit skilled staff
- improve productivity
- extend labour market
- reduce space costs, cut overheads, avoid relocation
- reduce travel time
- improved customer service
- improved computer awareness (eg in field staff)
- reduction of stress in staff
- elimination of transport problems

They then turn to consider the downside of teleworking.

Disadvantages as perceived by employer:
- communication difficulties
- management control problems
- motivation and discipline
- unavailability for meetings
- social isolation (affecting performance)
- lack of commitment to organisational goals and culture

- reliability costs of hardware, software and communications
- training costs
- loss of face-to-face contact
- assessing suitability of job
- assessing suitability of staff
- deciding on suitable equipment

"The main disadvantages for the employer relate to loss of control in a broad sense. Some concerns are raised regarding discipline and motivation, but also about difficulties in socialising workers into the firm and promoting commitment to organisational goals and culture," the report summarised.

The issue of telework obviously raises quite fundamental questions relating to an employee's relationship with their employer. The question which I wanted to consider, as I headed for Scotland, was whether companies who choose to introduce flexible working methods like teleworking also want to transform the formal, legal, employment relationship which they have with their staff.

References

1 *Teleworking: BT's Inverness experience* [511/studies/tech/rep/007 - version 1] 1994.

2 *Teleworking Explained* by Mike Gray, Noel Hodson and Gil Gordon, John Wiley and Sons, 1993.

   Other publications include: *Corporate Teleworking, The Competitive Advantage for the Future* by John Withnell, BT, 1991; *Managing Teleworking* by Gil Gordon, BT, February 1994; *The Economics of Teleworking* by Noel Hodson, BT, n.d.; *A Study of the Environmental Impact of Teleworking* by M H Lyons, BT, December 1990; *A Study of Homeworking Environments* by David Tucknutt, BT, April 1992.

3 *Conditions of Work Digest*, vol 9, 1/1990. Telework. International Labour Office, Geneva.

4 *Teleworking in Britain*. A report to the Employment Department by Ursula Huws, Analytica, Employment Department, research series no 18, October 1993.

5 *Review of Telework in Britain: Implications for Public Policy*. Prepared for the Parliamentary Office of Science and Technology by Andrew Gillespie, Ranald Richardson and James Cornford, Centre for Urban and Regional Development Studies, University of Newcastle upon Tyne, February 1995.

Journey 4

Blairgowrie and Helensburgh

Crossaig Ltd: the telework company

Crossaig Ltd is something unusual: a commercial company which, from its start-up in 1990, has had most of its employees teleworking from home.

I had arranged to visit Rosemary Rattney in Blairgowrie, a few miles north of Perth on the edge of the Scottish Highlands. Rosemary is one of Crossaig's longest-serving employees, having been working as a medical indexer for the company since August 1991. She currently works about three and a half days a week – though at a push she says she can get through the week's allocation of work in three days flat – and estimates that she can earn up to £17.50 an hour.

But first, however, I had gone to Helensburgh, the pleasant town overlooking the estuary of the river Clyde, to meet Crossaig's General Manager Tim Blaxter. The company's head office, a detached house just off Helensburgh's main shopping streets, is base for about 18 people, including the company's senior management. But the company's remaining 40 or so employees live and work elsewhere in Scotland, frequently many long hours' driving away from Helensburgh. Most, like Rosemary Rattney, work part-time from home.

Crossaig's business is rooted in the opportunities offered by information and communications technology. Its main clients are electronic database publishers, and the main business is preparation of new entries for these databases from specialist scientific and technical journals. For example, Crossaig currently provides about 100,000 new entries a year for the leading biomedical database EMBASE, published by the Dutch company Elsevier (now part of the Reed-Elsevier group). EMBASE contains many millions of abstracts and citations of articles from well over 4,000 medical journals published around the world.

Crossaig's work in producing these abstracts and citations, from hard-copy editions of the journals which are sent by carrier to Helensburgh, makes extensive use of technology. All journal text is electronically scanned by high-speed scanners, and then converted using optical character recognition (OCR) into editable text files. These files are then sent around Scotland to Crossaig's teleworkers, delivered to their homes by BT Integrated Services Digital Network lines. ISDN is essential for the company's work organisation. According to Tim Blaxter, the time taken to download a page image is reduced from about 15 minutes (using a conventional telephone line and modem) to about 15 seconds. Crossaig pays BT's current £400 installation charge for each individual ISDN line.

There are two main aspects to the work of producing database entries from this electronic raw material. Crossaig (which is now part of the international Thomson Corporation) employs a team of staff to extract the abstract normally published with each journal article, a relatively straightforward task. However, the company also employs more specialist staff with medical or scientific knowledge necessary to produce indexes for the journal articles. Indexers, like Rosemary Rattney, are paid on a piecework basis, with rates ranging from 90p to £2.25 per article.

Crossaig's chief executive Huw Baynham, one of the company's founder directors, set up the company after a stint with the Scottish Development Agency, at a time in the late 1980s when there was interest in Scotland in the emerging possibilities of teleworking technology for economic development. There is perhaps a lingering suspicion that one of the motives behind Crossaig has been a determination to prove that it can be done – that a successful new start-up can be built around teleworking staff. Huw Baynham has argued, however, that this way of working best serves Crossaig's business interests:

"We see significant advantage in continuing this policy of using devolved staff. The flexibility that it provides is important to us *and* our staff ... We are very happy with the efficiency of the processing that devolved working can lead to, set against normal office-based activities."[1]

Tim Blaxter elaborates on this argument. "We are adding value by indexing articles by using very specialist indexers, many of them with PhDs. Because we use teleworkers, we can recruit people with the expertise," he says. The necessary number of, say, pharmacologists or marine biologists won't necessarily happen to live within commuting distance of Helensburgh, in other words .

Tim Blaxter adds that cost savings is not the main motivation. Indeed, he says: "There should be recognition that teleworking is not necessarily a cheap option". Certainly, there is the expense of installing ISDN lines to all staff. Crossaig's method of working also means that one of the firm's senior staff spends a large amount of his time on the road, visiting isolated teleworking employees. In strict cost-benefit terms, it seems a dubious use of management time.

The visits are welcomed, however, by Rosemary Rattney as a way of keeping in touch with her employer. Her home is more than eighty miles from Helensburgh, and she has been to the company's head office only three times in the four years, once for a meeting and twice for staff parties. These social occasions are not something she particularly enjoys, she says: she only knows a handful of other Crossaig staff at all well.

Despite her length of service with the company, she admits that her relationship with Crossaig is not a very close one. But the work itself, and the opportunity to telework from her home, she clearly finds satisfying. "I answered an obscure advert in the Glasgow Herald, which said something like 'we are a company looking for people with medical or pharmaceutical experience and who can work with computers'," she says. "I showed the advert to my husband and he said, 'phone them up and find out more'. Initially I couldn't get an ISDN line installed here, but I badgered Crossaig and eventually rented an office in Perth. In July 92 BT put a line in here."

Work is fitted in with the rest of her life, including the needs of her two children, aged 11 and 9. This usually means working from about 9am, as soon as the children have been taken to school and the dog walked, until about 3.10pm when it is time for the afternoon school run. When necessary, however, Rosemary fits in an early stint from 6.30am to 7.45am, and works for another hour later in the afternoon. "I almost never work weekends," she says.

"It's a very isolated way of working, and in some respects I miss human contact. But as long as you make an effort to make social contact outside work, it's OK," she adds.

Whilst the majority of Crossaig's staff telework from home, the company has experimented with other arrangements. As we have already seen, some extractors and indexers work from the Helensburgh office. There is also a cluster of employees living in the immediate vicinity of Lochgilphead, a small settlement in Argyll at the head of the peninsula of Kintyre. Crossaig has opened a small office with three workstations in Lochgilphead, available for employees who want to use its facilities, and also arranges for one staff member there to undertake coordination tasks, at £4.50 an hour.

"We are not in teleworking as a social service, and if it became unprofitable we'd change the arrangements," says Tim Blaxter. But he adds, "We are employing people in remote areas doing clever work, using their minds, keeping up to date and contributing to their local society. And we are able to satisfy our customers. I get a tremendous kick from this."

One of Crossaig's management principles is that its staff should be employees, with formal employment contracts, rather than self-employed freelances. As Huw Baynham has said: "We have recently gone through a major exercise to establish 'good' contracts with all our staff to reflect the way in which they work. We spend a lot of time attempting to 'bind' our remote staff fully into the organisation."[2]

This means, for example, that the company offers sick pay and life insurance provision to its teleworkers, though there is no holiday pay entitlement. The company also offers limited remuneration if work is temporarily unavailable or if there are technical problems in sending it out to teleworkers. Staff who are unable to work for these reasons for five consecutive days are paid half of average earnings (this arrangement continues for up to four weeks).

It has to be added, however, that Crossaig also subcontracts some of its work, both to an Aberdeen-based business EBD Associates and to a group in the Western Isles. Workers undertaking Crossaig work on a subcontracted basis are not protected with employee status.

The issue of employment status is something which needs to be considered further, in the more general context of the development of telework in Britain. What I have called the 'classic' telework scenario is based on the assumption that the teleworker will be an employee of their company who just happens to have their work location at home rather than in an office. This has certainly been the model, as we have seen, used by BT in Inverness and Southampton, as well as by Crossaig. Anyone reading the copious literature reviewing some of the other corporate exponents of home-based teleworking in Britain will know that other companies, such as ICL and its subsidiary CPS, give their teleworkers employee status.[3]

But this has by no means been the whole story. The first major British experiment in this way of working was Rank Xerox's scheme in the early 1980s to encourage over 50 staff to become 'networkers', working partly for their old company and partly for other clients. Part of the condition of the arrangement was that the 'networkers' left Rank Xerox's employment (indeed, the company went further: perhaps concerned that the Inland Revenue might take an interest in the arrangement, Rank Xerox insisted that each person set up their own limited company rather than trading as self-employed sole traders).

A generally upbeat report of the 'networking' scheme in 1985 suggested that most of the ex-employees were happy with the arrangement. But even those whose businesses were developing successfully commented on the change in their employment status. "You quickly realise how vulnerable you are compared to your old situation, and the protection offered to you through what are regarded as standard terms of employment for large companies. It suddenly becomes obvious how valuable pensions, insurance, sick pay, holiday pay and BUPA are!" wrote the first networker, Roger Walker.[4]

Another British company with early experience of using home-based staff has been the FI Group (formerly F International), which developed primarily by making use of self-employed 'panel members'. The 'F' of its name originally stood for 'freelance'.

Given the restructuring which many companies have engaged in in recent years – including the shedding of staff through downsizing programmes, the reduction in the number of management layers and the increased contracting-out of non-core business functions – it is perhaps surprising that there has been as much corporate interest as there has been in teleworking programmes for employees. It might seem to be more in the interests of firms who have got as far as considering flexible teleworking arrangements to go one step further, and to review also the contractual relationship with the individual teleworker – in other words, to shed not only the task of providing the workplace but also the employer's responsibilities.

As anyone who has been self-employed knows, making your own work and running your own business can be a stimulating and profitable experience but it can also be fraught with dangers. Writers on management issues and the future of work may tell us that the days of the job for life have gone for ever, but there is no doubt that most people still prefer the residual protection that comes from having a formal employment contract and a regular day when the wage or salary payment arrives.

This certainly seems to have been the lesson of a Californian case in the mid 1980s, when a group of former employees of a life insurance company which had encouraged them to become self-employed teleworkers began suing their old employer. The case, as reported in the American journal *Across the Board*, was as follows:

"In 1982, California Western States Life Insurance Company offered some of its insurance-claims processors the opportunity to do their work at home instead of in the office. They would become contractors, paid by a piece rate and given no benefits. The processors, most of them women with family responsibilities, saw it as an attractive option at first. They could have more flexibility and save the money and time previously spent commuting. Most of them joined the program in 1983.

"On December 1st, 1985, eight of the women quit their jobs and filed a suit against the company, claiming that the independent contracting arrangement was simply a subterfuge to avoid paying them benefits."[5]

The story ended after three years, in May 1988 when the company was reported to have settled with its former employees out of court for an undisclosed sum. (A few months earlier, the insurer had also dropped its use of teleworking.)[6]

Whilst this story is interesting in pointing up the risks to individual teleworkers of forfeiting employee status, it is perhaps not directly relevant to the situation in Britain. Indeed, British employers might have more to fear from an Inland Revenue challenge to the assumption that individuals were self-employed rather than employees (and with it a claim from the Revenue for back income tax and National Insurance payments) than from any legal action by the teleworkers themselves. In any case, the removal of many employment rights in the series of legislative changes to UK employment law since 1979, and the British government's decision not to accept the EU's Maastricht agreement on social policy, means that companies have fewer obligations to their employees than in the past. Offering a teleworker employment status may increase the opportunity for managerial control, without necessarily greatly increasing the employer's contractual responsibilities to the individual.

Many of these issues are discussed in the guide to telework management published in May 1995 by the Department of Employment.[7] The guide summarises much that has become best practice in existing telework projects (such as BT's initiatives in Inverness and Southampton) and offers detailed advice for companies considering using teleworkers. "Drawing up contracts for teleworkers can seem a daunting task. But in practice it presents problems only in a minority of cases," it says reassuringly.

Where is the role of trade unions, the traditional mechanism used by employees to defend their collective interests, in these developments? In general, British unions who have developed policies on teleworking have been concerned to stress the importance of ensuring the maintenance of employment status for teleworking staff. For example, the first two points on a checklist for good practice for telework, drawn up by the white-collar union MSF are that:

Home-based working should always be voluntary,

Home-based workers should be employees (enjoying full employment rights) and not self-employed subcontractors.[8]

According to MSF's Bill Walsh, however, unions should not reject the idea of telework per se:

"There are good and bad employers and there will be those who will use the new technologies to offer new services to business and who will employ people on poor pay and in unsatisfactory conditions, without safeguards. However, for trade unions, a knee jerk reaction based on the experience of the worst cases is not a sufficient response ... MSF is campaigning to ensure that home-based working is a genuine extension of freedom for people at work and that it does not become a lonely prison ... The union wants to see a wide range of employment opportunities being made available to the home-based teleworker, and not just low paid, routine tasks which carry no career prospects."

MSF's checklist for good telework practice goes on to include a number of other points, which can be summarised as follows:

- safe working environment;
- regular opportunities for teleworkers to meet other colleagues and managers;
- access to electronic mail and telephone links to each other;
- responsibility of managers to keep in regular contact;
- same rates of pay and employment benefits as office-based employees;
- teleworkers should be included in career development programmes;
- equipment used should be supplied and maintained by the employer;

- extra costs (heating, lighting, etc) should be met by the employer;
- employer responsibility for health and safety;
- teleworker representation on health and safety committees;
- same trade union rights as office-based employees,
- right of teleworkers to return to previous employment arrangements if they wish.[9]

Clearly, as the nature of work changes there are challenges both to trade unions' traditional role in the workplace and to the means used to recruit and involve the membership. However, unions may be able to find themselves a new role as membership organisations supplying the sort of work-related services – including professional advice in legal, health and safety, financial and technical issues – which dispersed teleworkers require. (If trade unions do not reach out to provide these services, there are others who will be happy to do so commercially.)

The technology is there to enable individual home-based workers to communicate with each other and develop a collective voice. Already, for example, the National Union of Journalists and the media union BECTU have combined forces to provide a members' on-line service, offering E-mail, bulletin boards and Internet access. Unison has also developed an E-mail service and has recently launched its own World Wide Web site.

References

1 Huw Baynham, E-mail message to Telework discussion list, 29 January 1995.

2 See note 1 above.

3 Anyone wanting access to British telework case studies already has a wide choice of reading. Among sources are:

[for ICL and CPS]: *The Telecommuters* by Francis Kinsman, John Wiley and Sons, 1987; *Telework: Towards the Elusive Office* by Ursula Huws, Werner B Korte and Simon Robinson, John Wiley and Sons, 1990; *Teleworking: Flexibility for a Few* by Andrew Wilson, Institute of Manpower Studies, 1991; 'Managing Home-based Software Staff' by Jane Smewing in *Teleworking – Real Business Benefits*, proceedings of British Computer Society seminar, 9 October 1991.

[for Lombard North Central]: *Teleworking Explained* by Mike Gray, Noel Hodson and Gil Gordon, John Wiley and Sons, 1993.

[for Mercury]: *Flexible Working with Information Technology: the business opportunity* by Mandy Lavery and Alison Templeton, Ovum, 1993.

[for Bull]: Andrew Wilson, op cit, 1991.

[for Digital] Andrew Wilson, op cit, 1991; *Telework: the Human Resources Implications* by John and Celia Stanworth, IPM 1991.

[for Solicitors Complaints Bureau]: Andrew Wilson, op cit, 1991.

[for Royal Borough of Windsor & Maidenhead]: *Teleworking, a Strategic Guide for Management* by Steven Burch, Kogan Page, 1991.

[for FI]: Ursula Huws et al, op cit, 1990; Francis Kinsman, op cit, 1987.

[for Rank Xerox]: Ursula Huws et al, op cit, 1990; Francis Kinsman, op cit, 1987; *Networking in Organisations: the Rank Xerox Experiment*, by Phillip Judkins, David West and John Drew, Gower, 1985.

4 *Networking in Organisations: the Rank Xerox Experiment* by Phillip Judkins, David West and John Drew, Gower, 1985.

5 'A Hard Day's Work in the Electronic Cottage', Kathleen Christensen in *Across The Board*, April 1987.

6 See *Business Week* (international edition), 10 October 1988, p 43.

7 *A Manager's Guide to Teleworking*, written by Ursula Huws on behalf of the Employment Department, n.d. [1995].

8 *The Best of Both Worlds: Teleworking – A Trade Union Perspective* by Bill Walsh, MSF, 30 September 1993. Similar points were raised by David Souter, formerly head of research for the National Communications Union (now merged into the CWU), in a presentation to the DTI Teleworking special interest group conference, December 1994.

9 See note 8 above.

Journey 5

Forres

Outsourcing in the Highlands

Park on a yellow line in the London Borough of Newham, in nearby Tower Hamlets, or across the city in the boroughs of Ealing or Brent, and when you ring up to complain about the parking ticket on your windscreen the person answering the phone will almost certainly have a Scottish accent.

More precisely, the local rate 0345 number you will have been given as a contact line will have transferred you to a new purpose-built industrial unit on the edge of Forres in north-east Scotland, 26 miles east of Inverness. Inside, staff working for the IT consultancy and software company Hoskyns will already have access to your details. Each parking attendant (not 'traffic warden' any longer, please note) tramping the streets of these London boroughs has been provided with a hand-held computer which issues the tickets. Each night the day's haul is downloaded electronically, available for processing at the Forres centre.

The geographical – and perhaps also cultural – distance between, say, the streets around Petticoat Lane and the edge of the Moray Firth might seem to constitute a considerable barrier to this operation. In fact, Hoskyns says that the arrangement should be completely unnoticeable to users. For example, staff in Forres answer the phone in the name of the relevant London Borough. They have also been trained on what to say to callers who are keen to discuss the exact place on the local High Street where the parking ticket was issued: "We say, sorry, we're not in the area. We don't say, actually we're 600 miles away," says Les Morgan, General Manager of Hoskyns' Forres operation.

Hoskyns opened their processing centre in Forres in April 1994, and expanded early in spring of 1995 to a neighbouring purpose-built unit. It is a business which is growing fast. When I visited, the number of employees had reached about 45. But Les Morgan was preparing to recruit again, and his new building was built to accommodate up to 200. The target for 1998, he told me, was to have 1,000 staff in post, spread across about five sites in the north of Scotland.

Hoskyns' business at Forres is based on taking subcontracted work from other companies. The fashionable term used to describe this process is 'business process outsourcing' or BPO. The theory is that companies should concentrate on their core business activity, passing out their back-office administrative and information processing work to other firms – firms like Hoskyns for whom this is their core activity.

For example, Hoskyns suggests that whilst companies need to retain control over their decision-making and 'judgemental' processes (such things as management strategy, sales and marketing and corporate image), they can outsource much of the rest of their activity: everything from dealing with correspondence and telephone calls to letter production and company mailings.

In the case of parking tickets for the four London boroughs, Hoskyns handles enquiries from motorists (both post and telephone), processes payments of fines made by post or by credit card and initiates the legal processes for anyone who fails to pay up in the set time. The boroughs themselves are responsible for establishing parking policy and handling the court cases. (A third company, Sterling Granada, employs the parking attendants.)

Hoskyns' opportunity for this business follows the passing of the Road Traffic Act of 1991, which gave the London boroughs responsibility for most of the parking enforcement work in their areas (the Act came into effect in July 1994). Whilst the police continue to deal with parking offences on main trunk roads, other roads are no longer their responsibility and instead 1,200 parking attendants patrol in their place. "Under the new system, it is anticipated that the number of tickets issued will double," Hoskyns says cheerfully.

Hoskyns' unit at Forres also has contracts from two Scottish local authorities to administer aspects of council tax benefit and housing benefit claims. Grampian, for example, has arranged for new claims for council tax benefit in Aberdeen to be outsourced to the company. Applications from claimants and evidence such as wages slips and bank statements sent by them to support their claims are scanned into a computer database, accessible both by the authority and by Hoskyns staff.

There are clearly other potentially fruitful opportunities ahead for Hoskyns and its competitors in the outsourcing business. Les Morgan talks of the prospects of undertaking the billing work for privatised gas and electricity utility companies: "Does an organisation whose business is the delivery of gas or electricity really want to do all the billing?" he asks.

There is no secret why this work is gravitating geographically to places like Forres. Les Morgan says that in general his building costs are a fifth of those in London while staff costs, he adds, are half those of London. What this means translated into figures is that Hoskyns' employees in Forres earn about £8,500 a year. About 70 per cent of the current staff are women.

There is also public money available to create employment. Despite its image as a comfortably respectable town, Forres' registered unemployment levels have been high. Helpfully, the town happens to fall both within the area covered by Highlands and Islands Enterprise (formerly the Highlands and Islands Development Board) and Grampian Regional Council, both keen to support economic development in their areas. Hoskyns has become a key plank in the strategy of creating jobs in rural Scotland.

In some ways, Hoskyns' arrival in the north of Scotland can be taken as evidence that the Highlands and Islands Development Board was correct in its thinking in the late 1980s, when it put considerable stress on the importance of developing the telecommunications infrastructure of the area. The Highlands and Islands, stretching from Shetland to the Mull of Kintyre, comprises one sixth of the UK landmass but has only about 370,000 people, giving it one of the lowest population densities in the European Union.

"It became apparent from early discussions with British Telecom that the existing telecommunications network was wholly inadequate for modern purposes, without fibre optics, digital exchanges, even kilostream. Furthermore BT had no plans to upgrade the network in the area. The prospective commercial return on the large investment from such a sparsely populated area was too low to justify the expenditure. Left to commercial forces, the new services were unlikely to come to the Highlands and Islands for another 20 years, last as usual in the UK queue!" says David Henderson, HIE's head of projects and research.[1]

Instead the Highlands and Islands Development Board and BT jointly agreed to collaborate on the Highlands and Islands Initiative (now more frequently referred to as the Highlands and Islands Telecommunications Initiative), a project designed to install a sophisticated new telecoms network across much of northern Scotland, providing digital exchange services and access to dedicated lines for data transmission. For example, about 80 per cent of businesses in the area now have access to ISDN lines.

The Initiative involved an expenditure of approaching £20 million, of which about £5 million was public money, routed via the HIDB. It was seen at the time of its launch in 1989 as an attempt to overcome the geographical disadvantages of the area. "Information technology will unlock a huge field of commercial opportunities for the north of Scotland and render distance from markets irrelevant," said HIDB's then Chairman Sir Robert Cowan at the launch. "Without doubt, this is the most important single investment the HIDB has made in the economic future of the Highlands and Islands."[2]

From the start of the Initiative, the HIDB stressed the new opportunities provided for teleworking and remote working in the north of Scotland. There was also an emphasis on encouraging community-based use of the technology. HIDB, and then HIE, has supported the development of a number of Community Teleservice Centres, following the model which has more generally become known elsewhere in Britain as telecottages, and four pilot CTCs were established in Unst, Hoy, Islay and Lochgilphead. There has also been use made of the opportunities of the technology by schools and other educational bodies in the area.

However, six years on, there is perhaps a feeling that not all the initial hopes of the Highlands and Islands Initiative have been met. There is also the practical reality that the Highlands and Islands' lead has slipped: most of the rest of Britain now has had its telecoms infrastructure upgraded, and the time when parts of northern Scotland were ahead of central London for ISDN facilities has long gone.

The use made by business of the Initiative's telecoms infrastructure was the subject of a 1994 report by Andrew Gillespie and Ranald Richardson. They painted a mixed picture, concluding that existing businesses in the region have made little use of the technology:

> "It is clear from research interviews that it has proved extremely difficult to translate the provision of advanced infrastructure into the use of advanced services by regional enterprises. The uptake by the private sector in the region, particularly by SMEs (small and medium-sized enterprises), appears to have been low. The issue is an extremely sensitive one to the Initiative sponsors, and no usage figures have been made public; nevertheless, one interviewee admitted that 'the existing infrastructure is massively under-utilised'."

However they stressed the Initiative's role as a catalyst in encouraging companies like Hoskyns to base back-office units in the area:

> "For the future, call centres and back offices in particular appear to show marked growth potential. 'Teleworking' in the Highlands and Islands will, therefore, primarily be undertaken from conventional offices (ie work-places), usually located in the main regional population centres. The image of the self-employed professional teleworker operating from his (usually his) home-office in a remote glen may be a seductive marketing image, but it is unlikely to represent the reality for the majority of Highland teleworkers."[3]

HIE claimed in 1994 that over 350 jobs had been created over the previous three years as a result, directly or indirectly, of the advanced telecoms network installed. The subsequent opening of Hoskyns in Forres has added to the total. Les Morgan says that the access to good telecommunications facilities is essential for his company's operations.

In fact, Hoskyns could have been in David Henderson's mind when he summed up the benefits of the telecoms Initiative:

> "Telecommunications are a liberating force, freeing businesses from previous constraints, and allowing them to access the attractive and lower cost resources available in the Highlands and Islands. Principal amongst these is the quality of the workforce which can be obtained … Amongst the female population in particular there are large reserves of under-utilised education and ability, eager for employment. The commitment which these people have to living in their own community means that employers benefit from a high degree of loyalty and very low turnover of staff."[4]

Taking a more general perspective than simply that of northern Scotland, distance working using information and communications technologies – my definition of teleworking – clearly provides new opportunities for employment for rural and remote areas. But it is obviously important to ensure, as the Highlands and Islands Initiative largely did, that the telecoms facilities are adequate. There is also an ongoing requirement to ensure that the infrastructure continues to be upgraded.

That this is more of a political than a technological issue is reflected in the debate within the European Union over arrangements for continuing with the provision of universal telecoms service once the existing public telecoms monopolies in EU member states have been 'liberalised'. In a market-led telecoms market, why should a small number of users in, say, a remote mountain area have access to the same telecoms facilities as users in a large city?

The EU's current thinking on this sensitive issue emerged early in 1995 with the publication of the second part of a Green Paper on telecoms liberalisation in member states. The Green Paper proposes that telecoms companies' requirements to provide universal service should, at least initially, be limited to conventional voice telephony services. The Green Paper's preference was for the creation of a fund, paid for by levies from telecoms operators, to meet the costs of universal service.

However this issue is eventually resolved, it is clear that the technological possibilities for remote working for rural areas may be offset by the higher costs of accessing the technology. In other words, the development of this sort of teleworking depends on political decisions related to telecoms provision, rather than on the technology itself.

There is one aspect of Hoskyns' operation at Forres which we have not yet considered. Technologically, there is no reason why the company could not make use of home-based teleworkers – or perhaps teams of teleworkers located in the Highlands and Islands' Community Teleservice Centres – to undertake its work. Whilst there would be extra costs, there would also be considerable savings in the overheads.

Les Morgan is adamant, however, that he would not consider home-based staff, and he adds that he has turned down suggestions from telecottages that he might want to subcontract work on to them. His reason is interesting: "The whole benefit of working from here is the team work we can develop, the office atmosphere, and the culture created". Particularly important is the culture of customer care which he is trying to inculcate among his employees.

This is not a conventionally managed office. There is an emphasis on informality, which includes informal dress. "All members of staff are on first name terms and have direct access to all levels of the hierarchy. Regular 'open access' sessions are held in which views may be aired and opinions voiced openly," says the company.[5]

In fact, the management structure is extremely flat with only two intermediate levels (team leaders and 'customer care assistants') between Les Morgan and the bulk of his workforce. There are rituals which he has developed, as bonding mechanisms: all staff have sprigs of white heather, for example, to wear on days when potential new customers are visiting the building. And Les Morgan has asked the whole workforce to collectively devise the office's statement of values, prominently displayed throughout the building (these include 'being part of a team', 'attention being paid to quality' and 'people willing to try new ideas without being put down'; there is a converse list of 'do not' values which include 'messages not being passed on', 'good work being ignored' and 'colleagues who think the public are a nuisance').

There are other unusual aspects to being a Hoskyns' employee at Forres. Just before my visit, Les Morgan had presented all his staff individually with a paperback copy of Ricardo Semler's book *Maverick*, a provocative account of Semler's radical management strategy at his Brazilian company Semco. Semler's practice has become well-known in current debates on management and he is now a regular speaker on the lecture-circuit. An extract from *Maverick* gives a taste of his ideas:

> "Today, our factory workers sometimes set their own production quotas and even come in on their own time to meet them, without prodding from management or overtime pay. They help redesign the products they make and formulate the marketing plans …"[6]

Clearly, Les Morgan feels that Semler has something to say to his own staff at Forres as they cope with abusive telephone calls from motorists objecting to their parking tickets.

The management ideas at Forres are interesting not just in themselves, however. New forms of working clearly raise new issues of management, as the existing literature on telework makes clear.

Technology permits today much greater insight by management into employees' exact work performance than in the past. As we have already seen, Margaret Birkett had access to comprehensive statistics on the work being carried out in Southampton by her BT staff, both at home and in the call centre. Keyboard use is particularly easy to measure: a writer reporting on the word processing unit developed in the northeast of England by one of the big clearing banks quoted a bank official as saying: "We could actually measure productivity from London on the computer system. We actually know who are the most productive secretaries: we know the number of key strokes they do per hour or per minute."[7]

But much of the literature written for companies planning telework programmes has stressed the need to move from management by supervision (checking exact hours worked by employees, for example) to management by results.

Old management styles, it is suggested, have no place in the more flexible working arrangements which are developing, of which teleworking is a particular example. Charles Handy in *The Age of Unreason*, for example, speaks of a need to reward good performance rather than punish the bad. "Intelligent people prefer to agree rather than to obey," he says, though he also warns: "Do not look to the new intelligent organisations with their intelligent machines and their cultures of consent for days of gossipy coffee breaks or for boring but untaxing jobs."[8]

I suspect that participative management styles and more democratic forms of work organisation are generally welcomed by most people – almost everyone, given the opportunity, wants to be able to do the best they can at work. (Whether collective value statements, group discussions and team building exercises change the fundamental relationship of an employee selling their labour to an employer is perhaps a different matter.)

But this is not just a matter of being nicer to employees. There is a business imperative involved too. It is clearly profitable to add as much value as possible to work undertaken, particularly in the case of outsourced information processing, where much of the work is relatively simple and easily automated. Hoskyns' quest for a high level of customer care is a search to add extra value to its operations.

And without this the work might not have ended up in Forres. After all, if work for London clients can be undertaken in Forres where overheads are much cheaper, why not send the work somewhere else where costs, especially labour costs, are even cheaper? Somewhere like India or the Philippines, perhaps.

"Basic data processing can be done much more cheaply in Delhi. The bottom end of the market will go to wherever in the world is the cheapest. It is the top end of the market, the value-added end, which we have to keep in Britain," says Les Morgan.

References

1 *Advanced Telecommunications, Remote Working and Regional Development*, paper by David M Henderson at European ISDN User Forum, 11-13 April 1994, Stockholm.

2 *Making the right connections into the future: the Highlands and Islands Initiative* (British Telecom) and Highlands and Islands Development Board press release 11/8/89, 'Seize your chance, businesses told'.
3 *Advanced Communications and Regional Development: The Highlands and Islands of Scotland* by Andrew Gillespie and Ranald Richardson, Centre for Urban and Regional Development Studies, University of Newcastle upon Tyne. Report undertaken as part of the ACCORDE Project [of the European Commission] within DG XIII's 'Telework 1994' initiative, August 1994.
4 See note 1 above.
5 *An Introduction to BPO*, Hoskyns.
6 *Maverick* by Ricardo Semler, Century, 1993.
7 Quoted in *Teleworking, a strategic guide for management* by Steven Burch, Kogan Page, 1991.
8 *The Age of Unreason* by Charles Handy, Business Books, 1989.

Journey 6

Cork

Call centres for the European market

We have become used to the idea of international trade in goods, and take no notice of the fact that our electrical appliances are built in Taiwan or our fresh vegetables imported from Kenya or Chile. We are not yet so used to the internationalisation of trade in services. But it has already arrived.

In a small office in an industrial estate in Mahon, on the outskirts of Cork city, the 15 or so women employed by Global-Res International Ltd are taking telephone reservations for hotels. The company handles the bookings for a number of chains of hotels, including the Ramada and Renaissance groups. The Cork office takes about 14,000 calls a month, checking availability and price and confirming reservations for hotel rooms worldwide.

Almost none of the telephone calls they receive in Cork come from callers in Ireland, however. Instead, the phone calls come in from one of about 15 countries elsewhere in Europe, or from Israel. In each case, the caller will be dialling a freephone number in their own country, which is then automatically routed to Cork. "The operation has to be transparent to the caller," says Cathal McCarthy, the operations manager for Global-Res in Cork.

This means of course that the telephone needs to be answered in the caller's own language. Global-Res's automated call distribution technology identifies the source of each incoming call, sending it wherever possible to a member of staff with the necessary language skills. Those women who speak more than one foreign language switch back and forth between, say, French and German as the calls come through.

Eavesdropping as I did at Global-Res one afternoon to the dozen or so phone conversations being carried on in the main call centre office is like listening in to the whole continent of Europe hard at work. The office is quiet, with the staff talking into headsets whilst checking data on PC screens in front of them. There is no babble of languages: only the quiet murmur and change of rhythm as one conversation in German finishes, another in French starts up whilst a few feet away a complicated hotel booking is being negotiated in Italian. According to Cathal McCarthy, his current team also includes staff who can speak Dutch, Spanish and Swedish.

The image of a group of women, mostly graduates in their early to mid-twenties, answering freephone calls from across Europe from an industrial estate in Cork is not the vision of Ireland most often promoted by the Irish tourist trade to foreign visitors. But Global-Res is not by any means unique. In fact, only about 500 yards down the road from Global-Res's Cork unit another group of call centre staff are doing almost identical work taking hotel reservations from across Europe for the Sheraton group. A third chain, Radisson Hotels International, has a call centre in Dublin, handling calls from 14 countries in 13 languages. Yet another group, Best Western Hotels, also has a call centre in Dublin.

It is not just hotel reservation work. South of Dublin in Bray, for example, the computer company Dell runs a 24-hour sales and technical support telephone service serving the whole of its European market. Dell employs about 270 people on this work.

A similar telesales and computer technical support operation is run by one of Dell's competitors, Gateway 2000, from a large plant north of Dublin. Gateway 2000 moved to Dublin two years ago, and after an initial foray into the UK and Irish market has now extended into France and Germany. The large open-plan office where the firm's telemarketing staff are based include English, French and German language sales teams.

There are other multinationals who have either opened or are planning telephone call centres like these in Ireland: the list includes Korean Air Lines (13 European countries served), the Japanese multimedia company Kao (16 countries) and a software support company Quarterdeck, where staff in Ireland also handle calls from North America outside US business hours.[1]

Their presence in Ireland is not accidental. It has much to do with a deliberate strategy by the Irish government's industrial development agency, IDA Ireland, to coax American companies to base their European telemarketing operations there. Brian Cogan, manager of industrial policy for Forfás (IDA Ireland's parent body), describes how he and Gus Jones, at that time a senior staff member from IDA Ireland's New York office, were given time off their previous jobs in 1991 and charged with exploring new areas where employment could be brought to Ireland. "We were particularly struck by the telemarketing industry," he says. "It is almost a mature industry in the US, with estimates that up to three million people are earning their living from it. It's very developed in the US compared with Europe, and the degree to which it is labour intensive was attractive to us." IDA Ireland's strategy quickly took shape: Ireland was to be offered as the telemarketing centre for the newly created European single market.

A joint IDA Ireland and Telecom Éireann sales brochure makes the case:

"Today Telemarketing and Teleservice are vital business tools ... By setting up your own Telemarketing or Teleservice operation in Ireland, you can share in the emergence of pan-European business ... Ireland, through Telecom Ireland, now offers amongst the least expensive international freefone numbers in Europe – and a comprehensive pricing package has been put in place to ensure that Ireland offers overseas companies fully competitive rates on all telecommunications service ..."[2]

The brochure goes on to describe another advantage for the parent company:"... Highly skilled and motivated young people are available at wage rates amongst the lowest in Europe ..."

The brochure's use of capital letters for 'telemarketing' and 'teleservice' suggests a certain hesitation as to whether these words can yet be assumed to be fully in the lexicographical mainstream. Both are generic terms for what is clearly something rather new: a range of work situations where humans (as employees or workers) interact with other humans (as customers or clients) using telephone technology, and backed up by computers.

Since business has been conducted by phone almost since the telephone was first invented, it is fair to ask what precisely it is that distinguishes this new type of work. In part it is the technology: the use being made, for example, of ACD (automated call distribution) switching, enabling high volumes of incoming calls to be sent out in orderly queues to waiting telephone operators. The use of computer technology is also important: what allows a hotel reservation centre to function, for example, is the access staff have to a worldwide computer database to check availability and make immediate reservations.

At the moment, the IT and telephony elements of the technology may not be linked: at Global-Res in Cork, for example, there is no technical integration between the incoming freephone calls and the data transmitted to and from the Ramada and Renaissance hotels reservations database (which happens to be located in Atlanta, and which is reached via a satellite dish on Global-Res's building).

Increasingly, however, the two technologies are merging. CTI, Computer Telephony Integration, is the term used by the industry to describe a wide range of developments which allow computer technology to support and enhance telephone calls. Already CTI has entered everyday life, with the growth of applications such as voice mail and computer-recognition of voice input by callers. For telemarketing, CTI promises much: one obvious use, for example, is the ability to bring up records of a caller on-screen as their call is answered, a process which has been called 'screen popping'.

But the work methods which are described by these terms 'telemarketing' and 'teleservice' are more than just a matter of technology. The work process itself has changed. In particular, there has been the development of the call centre, the anonymous base for the telemarketing operation which as we have already seen is much more likely to be on a low-cost industrial estate than in the prestigious (but expensive) public areas where offices used to be located.

The sorts of work which can be undertaken in a call centre are diverse. They include central reservation centres (such as Global-Res's operation), direct selling (as Dell and Gateway 2000 are undertaking), customer support and sales (such as BT's Volume Business Sales division) and technical support centres (again, as provided by the PC direct companies). Market research by telephone is another example.

Clearly, the development of directly sold insurance (pioneered in Britain by Direct Line, and now widely imitated) is another manifestation of the same phenomenon. So, too, is the type of home banking offered by First Direct, which again has been copied by many other banks (the Co-op, for example, services all its personal customers across Britain from a call centre in Skelmersdale).

The US has also seen a phenomenal growth in the use by manufacturers of 'care lines' – telephone numbers (usually tollfree) which are printed on supermarket goods which consumers can ring with complaints or questions. Over 80 per cent of branded goods in US supermarkets carry care line numbers. In Britain, by contrast, a report in March 1995[3] found that only about 22 per cent of goods offered care line back-up, though the report also noted that the market was growing fast. Care line provision is an obvious target for subcontracting out to specialist companies, in line with the business process outsourcing model.

Telemarketing has already become important in the perhaps unlikely context of charity fund-raising. Telephone fund-raising (now normally focused on known supporters or likely supporters of a cause) has developed into a mini-industry, mainly because it has been shown to be extremely effective in raising funds. Some charities have in-house telemarketing teams (ActionAid, for example, says it may make 100,000 telephone calls on a single project). Other charities, however, use specialist commercial telemarketing companies for this work. One Bournemouth-based firm, for example, recently advertised itself to charities as "the leading telemarketing agency for the sensitive and cost effective recruitment of volunteer collectors for house to house, street and home money box collections". Another talks of 'relationship marketing by telephone' (this means attempting to increase a supporter's sense of commitment to the cause).[4]

As in other areas of telemarketing the work involves the use of both telephone and computer technology, with staff normally using a preset script to guide the conversation with would-be donors. Not all practitioners are as professional as they might be. One established company recently complained of rogue firms where "phoners are given little or no training, and are typically expected to speak to 25 or more people in an hour ... they are typically paid on commission, and perhaps earn £1.50 to £2.00 an hour working from home".[5]

This brings us back to the question of what it is like to work in a telemarketing call centre. The answer, if we are honest, is not a very reassuring one. Unlike traditional office life where individual workers can pace themselves throughout the day, call centre technology selects and dictates the work to be done.

Cathal McCarthy at Global-Res is honest about this problem. "It is a very controlled environment, controlled by the ACD machine," he says. The management challenge is to find ways to combat this, and to reduce the attrition rate of staff leaving. "We try to make life more interesting. I'm sending people away to work for a time in hotels. We also have performance related rewards for people who reach certain sales targets. For example, the top three people each month are taken out for a meal."

Gateway 2000 in Dublin tries even harder. An *Irish Times* interview with one telesales worker there, Sylvia Kwik, explored some of the company's 'spiffs' – gimmicks used to whip up the sales staff into a suitable state of selling euphoria: "The company is very into spiffs, says Kwik ... Last week they put up balloons and every time we made a sale we went up and burst one and got the £1 coin inside. Recently we had a Seventies day and there were face painters in, so we were speaking to customers on the phone with paint on our faces while the video of *Grease* played in the background."[6]

This sort of event clearly helps both to sell more products and to humanise the workplace. If we stand back, however, to analyse what is involved in telemarketing in all its various shapes and forms, what emerges is a growing trend towards the dehumanisation of the work process. It's not an exaggeration to say that what is happening in these parts of the service sector today bears comparison with what happened a century and more ago in manufacturing. The mechanisation of manufacturing away from its original craft base, and in particular developments such as the use of assembly lines and the implementation of Taylorist forms of management, were made possible by technological change. A similar routinising and automation of office-based work processes is going on now. Call centres, it can be argued, are today's version of the assembly-line factories.

The telemarketing call centre in Ireland is also predominantly a young person's workplace. Global-Res has access each year to a pool of about 200 language graduates emerging each year from University College, Cork, and as we have seen is staffed almost entirely by women in their early to mid-twenties. Brian Cogan of Forfás accepts that the 2,000 or so jobs which IDA Ireland's telemarketing drive in the US plans to create by 1997 will be primarily jobs for the young – though in a country like Ireland with a large young population this is clearly important. "You probably wouldn't make a career out of it. The work is suitable for young people coming out of schools and universities, and they probably won't stay more than three or four years. But they will be gaining good selling experience," he says.

IDA Ireland's package of incentives for American companies includes one of the lowest rates of corporation tax (10 per cent) in Europe, guaranteed at least until the year 2010. There are also capital, employment and training grants available. The rules are designed where possible to create full-time rather than part-time jobs, to ensure that Irish nationals get most of them, and also to make sure that the jobs remain for a minimum period of time. But provided the rules are met, the grants are generous. IDA Ireland is coy about divulging exact information but one company says that, for them, the subsidy on offer works out at

£8,000 per job created in Dublin and £10,000 per job in places like Cork.

This is similar to the sort of annual wage which a call centre member of staff could expect to earn. Global-Res, for example, pays a starting salary to its graduates of about £8,500 per annum (though high personal tax rates in Ireland reduce this to a take-home wage of perhaps £400 a month). At some telemarketing sites the pay may be £7,000 a year.

But there are two threats on the horizon, even to lowly-paid employment such as this. The first is that technological development, particularly in Computer Telephony Integration, will eliminate the need for the human altogether. Already we are becoming used to using our telephone keypads, or simple voice commands, to navigate our way through menus of options when phoning some companies' telephone lines. This is increasingly happening in the US: the report on care lines, for example, found that over half of US care lines are now answered by a voice-activated or tone menu system.

The second threat takes us back to the start of this chapter, to the internationalisation of trade in services. Ireland is an attractive home for telemarketing in Europe partly because of its cheap labour costs. Brian Cogan hopes that in the future Irish call centre staff may be able to service not just the European market but the home US market too, though he says this is not an imminent development. The Irish accent is considered very acceptable in North America, he adds.

But labour is cheaper, much much cheaper, in other parts of the world and telemarketing is not bound by geographical boundaries. The task once again in finding and then keeping the new jobs is to keep up the quality of the service on offer, to add more value. IDA Ireland stresses the high quality of its education system, and the advantage of its people speaking the international business language, English.

Ireland can also make use of its image in the eyes of the world. Cathal McCarthy says that callers from continental Europe are often intrigued to find themselves calling Cork. Where necessary, stereotyped ideas of a rural, if damp, green island can be used to advantage: "If they ask what the weather is like in Cork, we tell them it's raining even if in fact it's sunny outside," says Cathal McCarthy, only half in jest. But ultimately, of course, this sort of sentiment won't by itself be enough to find and keep the jobs.

References

1 A comprehensive list was published in the Telecom Ireland publication for the US market *Global Lines*, Spring 1995.
2 *Your Direct Line to Cost Effective Telemarketing and Teleservice in the Single European Market …is Ireland*, brochure from IDA Ireland, 1993.
3 *The Careline Report* 1995 by the L&R Group.
4 See, for example the Telephone Fund-raising feature in *Third Sector*, 9 March 1995.
5 *Third Sector*, 6 April 1995.
6 *Irish Times*, 19 April 1994.

Journey 7
Cyberspace

I was standing admiring the view from about 18 floors up the Canary Wharf tower, describing my progress on this book to the technology editor of one of the newspapers now based there. I mentioned that I was in the middle of an extensive trip around the British Isles: northern Scotland, the west of Ireland, the English south coast and a few days in Wales. He raised a metaphorical eyebrow. "Doesn't all this rather negate the whole idea?" he said. "I thought teleworking was supposed to do away with the need to travel?"

Of course he was right. If telework is a way of eliminating geographical distance why was I spending so much time in my car, in airplanes, on boats?

If he had seen the office at home where this book has been written, he could have followed up with a supplementary question: why all the piles of books and articles? Why the cuttings files, the hard-copy printouts of reports, the paperwork spread over desks and floor? What chance for the digitised world of the information society, when even writers on the subject seem to rely on the printed word?

Of course, I would have responded, I have dipped and dived into cyberspace for the research for the book. Arrangements for meetings have been set up by E-mail. I have chatted about aspects of telework on-line with members of CompuServe's Telework Europa forum and downloaded articles and reports from the forum's extensive electronic library. I've accessed on-line databases for information. I've quoted (readers of the footnotes will already have noticed) a contribution from

Crossaig's chief executive originally posted to the telework discussion list on the Internet.

Yes, I've used some of the power of the technology – why, I even obtained the full text of the University of California, Davis, book on telecommuting by dropping in to UCD's computer via the Internet and extracting the relevant file straight to my home PC. (Does it weaken my case if I also admit that previously somebody had already lent me a copy of the same report, in conventional book form?)

If I am honest, I have to admit that most of my research has been undertaken in the old ways. I found more of use in the various business and academic libraries I visited in person than I tracked down in various virtual journeys. In some instances, where I had a choice, I even turned down the opportunity to research on-line from home: for example, my keyword searches for telework-related material in FT Profile (a database of full-text newspaper and magazine articles) and ABI/Inform (abstracts from business and academic journals) could have been done by my home PC but instead I chose to undertake the searches using a CD-ROM disc in a library. (There was a reason: it was cheaper that way.)

So my conclusion has to be that, at present, it is impossible to write a book like this about telework just by teleworking. But I accept that this could change fast. Writers may be able to find all the information they need by journeying up the infobahns and the avenues of cyberspace (not forgetting, in the process, to take time off for some virtual sightseeing).

The term 'information highway' has become associated with the US Vice-President Al Gore, who has pursued the idea of a national information infrastructure (NII) for the US. European Union countries are preferring to talk about the 'information society'. Both ideas rest on an analysis of the importance which high-speed communication links will play in the future health of our economic and cultural life.

Just as railways and motorways have been essential for Western societies' industrialisation and development to date, enabling both goods and people to be moved around quickly, so an equivalent comprehensive communications network will be necessary in the society of the near future, it is argued. The lives we will lead, at work and at home, will require the rapid transfer of enormous quantities of information fast. The building of this information highway – or, perhaps, highways, for there may be several core networks – will be as important as the construction a generation or more ago of the American interstate highways or the M1 and M6 in Britain.

What has been happening in Britain? The Labour Party set out its ideas for the Information Superhighway in a report in the summer of 1995, whilst the British government's views were set out in a command paper in November 1994 which summarised the challenge ahead as follows:

> "Every society in the world is confronted with opportunities and challenges arising from the convergence of communications, information technology, media technologies and services, and the development of multimedia. These, combined with cheaper telecommunications, provide the scope for many new applications, especially with high-capacity two-way ('broadband') communications technologies."[1]

Whilst we wait for the information superhighway(s) to arrive, we have in the meantime the Internet phenomenon. The Internet provides a possible prefigurative model of what the future may hold. Owned by no-one, the network has grown up organically over a number of years from its origins in the US military and now links large numbers of computers worldwide (many millions? – it's impossible to say).

There is such an obvious danger of hype when describing developments such as the Internet that it's possible to overcompensate and fail to acknowledge just how significant its growth has been. Even in the few months in which I was working on this book, much changed.

Back in the autumn of 1994, the Internet was something of a fashion accessory, the smart London people were rushing to Cyberia cafe to check out the cakes and 'Net surfing facilities, the first issues of consumer magazines dedicated to the Net were appearing on newsagents shelves and hypertext addresses (the http://... prefix to document addresses on the World Wide Web) were still something of a novelty in the broadsheet newspapers.

A few months on, the Internet has official government support. Indeed technology minister Ian Taylor has been urging British companies to embrace the technology. "I believe that the business use of the Internet is really taking off this year ... Driven by its potential for business enhancement and reduced costs it can become a new forum for business transactions," he told a conference in May 1995.

Not only that, but the DTI's press release from which I took this extract of Ian Taylor's speech was itself to be found on the Internet. And the press release finishes not only with contact phone numbers for DTI staff but also with the minister's E-mail address: taylor@mintech.demon.co.uk.

Something surely must be moving when government ministers and the civil service embrace cyberspace so enthusiastically, and apparently so quickly. It is less than a year since the first faltering steps, when the command paper *Creating the Superhighways of the Future* was put up on the Internet (and it may be a little unkind to mention, but it is nonetheless true, that the DTI press release proudly announcing this fact got the Internet address wrong).

In fact, businesses haven't been waiting for the urgings of ministers. Barclaycard launched a series of pages on the World Wide Web in January 1995. In May, J Sainsbury began a 'wine direct' service from its own WWW pages. A few days later, Tesco, Dixons, WH Smith and Great Universal Stores opened their doors in Britain's first electronic mall, this time choosing to use the UK Shopping Centre on CompuServe.

Of course, Britain is still far behind North America, where CompuServe subscribers were able years ago to buy such essentials of life as the Slam-Dunkers' indoor basketball set ('patented recoiling action'), the Las Vegas casino slot machine ('the exhilaration of a Las Vegas casino in your home') and the Griffo grill ('unique new rack for better, easier grilling').

Horace Mitchell and his colleagues who produced the 1992-3 Teleworking Study for the Department of Trade and Industry coined the term 'teletrade' to describe business undertaken over electronic networks. The report stresses the importance of teletrade in an analysis of telework development, and the lead taken by North American companies in developing the new business opportunities. Horace

Mitchell has written:

> "Some 6 million USA consumers already buy goods and services directly through networks such as CompuServe, Prodigy and their competitors, while other purchases that are not made directly on the network are influenced by information and messages received over networks. An important effect of 'information highways' is that buyers and sellers become less aware of each other's geographical whereabouts. In the future 'geography of work', teletrade will have just as great an impact on jobs as telework, possibly greater.
>
> "The US Government has a well developed and fast moving 'Electronic Commerce' initiative designed to make US companies expert at teletrade techniques. Europe is waiting (and hoping!) for similar activities to emerge."[4]

As I write, the Internet is in the throes of gradually turning commercial. This process involves certain technical challenges including ways of safeguarding the transmission of payments through the system, since at present the Internet is not a secure mechanism for sending credit card details, the obvious way to pay for goods ordered (and indeed for information accessed, too). There are also intriguing but stubborn problems around copyright and intellectual property rights in a new publishing medium, which still need sorting out.

But the payment issue is likely to be resolved very shortly. This will open up considerably more opportunities for the commercial exploitation of the technology. It also means that the present situation, where Internet users can surf the world at almost no cost and extract any information they fancy also free of charge, may be under threat.

There still seems plenty of energy left in the idea of an international, participative means of communication, however. Christina Lamb captured well (in a *Financial Times* lead piece) some of the Internet's current fascination:

> "Late at night when real-life friends are sleeping, I make a coffee and sit at my desktop computer in Boston, US, to begin travels in the

virtual world which may take me anywhere from an aid organisation in Bombay to a research station atop a volcano in Hawaii. Across the globe, millions are engaged in heated on-line discussion of everything from politics to Elvis sightings, swopping travel or business tips, or even conducting love affairs with people they have never met …

"In general users are not computer nerds or social misfits who prefer communicating with a screen rather than a person. They are ordinary people seeking electronic soul mates to meet on-line without barriers of racism, sexism or age, without facing crime on the streets, and with whom they can form a community …"[5]

The Internet's development has demonstrated that information and communication technologies have liberating potential. It is a good moment to return to the themes of this book. Up to now I have focused on commercial use and exploitation of the potential of teleworking. I want to move on to consider some of the community-based attempts to make use of the technology to create jobs and employment opportunities, especially through the creation of locally based telecottages. As we shall see, some of the tensions in the Internet between commercial and non-commercial objectives can be found in the world of telework, too.

References

1 *Creating the Superhighways of the Future: Developing Broadband Communications in the UK*, November 1994.
2 'Internet can become new forum for business', speech by Ian Taylor at Daily Telegraph Internet Conference, 4 May 1995.
3 *CompuServe* magazine, March 1990.
4 *Plenty of Work, Not Many Jobs?* by Horace Mitchell (Management Technology Associates), Version 1, January 1995.
5 'Yes, it's true. I was a Cybervirgin', Christina Lamb, *Financial Times*, 26/27 March 1994.

Journey 8

Kinawley, Co Fermanagh

Developing a telecottage

From Cork I travelled north, eventually crossing from the Republic into County Fermanagh fifteen miles or so from Enniskillen. The A4 road is quiet, but the A32 which I turned into just before Enniskillen is quieter still. When eventually I turned again, on to a small broad, I was beginning to worry about my directions. Then I spotted the sign: 'Telecottage'.

I had arrived at the hamlet of Kinawley. This would be a remote area, even without the extra distortions to economic and social life caused by the presence of the border only about a mile away to the south. The quality of much of the farmland is poor, and (for obvious reasons) tourism is relatively undeveloped. Belfast is two hours' drive away, Dublin is three hours by slow roads.

Sheila McCaffrey and her husband Michael were determined to bring work to Kinawley, the area where they both grew up. For over five years from 1988, they pursued the idea. "In the early days we had an awful lot of rejections," says Sheila. But eventually, in November 1993, the purpose-built single-storey building which houses Kinawley Integrated Teleworking Enterprise Ltd, or simply KITE, opened. It is equipped with about a dozen 486 PCs, laser printers, a flat bed scanner, fax machine and BT ISDN line (and a large quantity of children's books and toys).

The McCaffreys' plans involved a recognition of the potential which new technology was offering for remote working. Sheila McCaffrey, whose background is in accountancy and management, had for a time worked in Enniskillen for an employer based in Florida and had quickly appreciated the advantages of using a modem and fax machine. Jobs at Kinawley, she believed, could be created by teleworking for remote clients.

The total cost of establishing KITE was about £220,000, which the McCaffreys raised from a complicated mosaic of funders. The centre initially received funds to run an IT training programme for local women, under the New Opportunities for Women (NOW) programme of the European Social Fund. NOW funding also helped establish child care facilities, an integral part of the project. Capital costs were funded partly by the European Regional Development Fund and by a number of charitable trusts. Help with management costs were provided by other employment development bodies.

There was also money available from the Department of Agriculture, as part of the grant support offered to farmers wanting to diversify out of agriculture: the KITE building was built on about 1.5 acres of previously marginal farmland taken from Michael McCaffrey's 20 acre holding in the area. Michael himself designed it and oversaw the construction work in the summer of 1993.

Though the McCaffreys themselves own the building, KITE itself has been established as a community business and is legally incorporated as a company limited by guarantee, the most common method of incorporation for community and voluntary sector initiatives. However the McCaffreys stress that KITE has to be commercial in its approach to clients. "It has to be market-driven. The intention has always been to create real work for real clients, offering quality work, on time at a competitive price," says Sheila.

The first crunch-time for this policy came in the summer of 1994, less than a year after KITE opened. For the first few months, the centre had been able to provide IT training for local women, making use of the NOW funds. When the course and the money came to an end, KITE had to make the transition from a training project to a business generating enough income to be able to pay employees. In a sense, KITE had arrived at the point where telework rhetoric meets the real world.

The transition took place on 1st August 1994. Since then, KITE has had a payroll of 14, comprising eight teleworkers together with nursery staff for the attached day-nursery, a cook and a cleaner. The teleworkers, who are on an hourly rate of about £3.50, are also offered free child care facilities.

The story of KITE's planning and birth is a wonderful example of vision and determination being brought to fruition, and the McCaffreys point out with deserved pride that they have been one of the very few NOW projects to be able to offer jobs to trainees when the training courses have finished.

But clearly, in order to continue in the future, KITE has to find itself a business. Fourteen employees is a large workforce for what is effectively a start-up operation.

Sheila McCaffrey admits that it has not been easy to find the work. Understandably, KITE is trying to open up a new market where few others have gone before, and Sheila says that despite talking to numerous consultants and marketing specialists she has failed to find anyone with the experience to advise them. KITE's professional publicity brochure is couched in general terms ("KITE's teleworkers can help your business by providing skills and services to 'plug the gaps' – whatever or wherever they may be"). A separate leaflet offers a bewilderingly long list of the services KITE can offer, including compilation and management of databases, desk top publishing, telesales, conference management, translation services, computerised accounting and advertisement management. Whilst this could be construed as a cast-your-bread-upon-the-waters approach to marketing, it could also be read as revealing the problems KITE has had to face in identifying where the work is likely to come from.

In fact, one of the first contracts KITE received was from the Surrey-based Sandpiper Camping Holidays, who asked KITE to handle local enquiries for its brochures out-of-hours. But the contract which carried KITE through the early part of 1995 was a substantial one involving data manipulation for an American client. The work, which was being undertaken during my visit, involved rearranging on-screen text files of individual CVs into a standard format, suitable for incorporating into a database. This was primarily a cut-and-paste type operation, repetitive and relatively mundane work which arrived from the USA in hard-copy form (and so did not make use of KITE's ISDN facilities, installed by an initially reluctant BT after a certain amount of persuasion).

But, nevertheless, it was work. It came KITE's way as a result of a three-week visit by Sheila McCaffrey to the USA in the autumn of 1994, when she set out to find corporate clients who might be interested in outsourcing work to them. It perhaps helped that Sheila's sister lives in the US, providing her with a base for her mission and some initial leads. Nevertheless Sheila describes the hard work involved in knocking on doors and setting up meetings with potential clients. And though she came back with a contract, this outcome was by no means inevitable: Michael candidly admits that KITE was 'very lucky' to get the work.

From an English perspective, KITE's decision to go for the US market can seem both courageous and ambitious. But the Irish perspective is perhaps different, reflecting the closer family ties between the two continents born of nineteenth century emigration from Ireland. One result of the Irish diaspora is that horizons can be broader, a useful attribute at a time when telework is beginning to offer the potential of working across national frontiers.

We have already noted the considerable resources being allocated by the Irish government in its efforts to bring telemarketing jobs from America to Ireland. However, this follows an earlier drive by IDA Ireland in the late 1980s which successfully persuaded a number of American companies to relocate elements of their back-office data processing work to Ireland.

The story of these American satellite offices in Ireland is an intriguing one. For example, the remote County Kerry town of Castleisland (temptingly close to the beautiful tourist areas of Macgillycuddy's Reeks and the Ring of Kerry) is not the obvious place where you would look for an office of the New York Life Assurance Co. Nevertheless, about 40 people are employed in Castleisland on data processing work for the New York firm.

Similarly, Massachusetts Mutual Life has established an office in

Tipperary, the Great-West Life Assurance Co is in Kilkenny, McGraw-Hill Inc operates from Galway, the Travelers Companies from Castletroy in County Limerick and the Neodata Corporation from locations in County Kerry and County Limerick. The financial services firm Cigna has taken a factory unit in the small town of Loughrea, east of Galway city.

Cigna's operation in Loughrea offers an example of the sort of work carried out in these satellite offices. About 120 staff (almost all women) work for the firm, between them processing about 4,000 medical insurance claims each day. The claims come from US policy-holders, and can range from requests for refunds for routine visits to local doctors to claims for major hospital surgery. The paperwork is currently flown from JF Kennedy Airport in New York via Brussels to Shannon, and is then brought by courier to Loughrea. Cigna staff at Loughrea have direct access to the company's central databases through two optic fibre data lines to Hartford, Connecticut, and can process and authorise claims on-line.

Indeed, apart from the fact that it does not handle a customer help-line for telephone enquiries, Cigna's operation in the west of Ireland is identical to those of its thirteen other regional claims offices actually located in the States. John Lyons, production manager at Loughrea, says that the technology which makes this possible is taken for granted. The air-freighting arrangements also seem to work effortlessly – in five years, he recalls only two occasions when boxes have temporarily gone astray on their journey to Shannon. (The company is, however, now contemplating the transmission of claims forms electronically to Loughrea.)

The advantage to Cigna of basing its office in Ireland comes down once again to the savings available on labour costs (Loughrea's claims processors earn about half the US equivalent), and the low levels of staff turnover. "It may not be an obvious thing to do to fly paperwork around the world, but claims processing is a fairly labour-intensive process and employee turnover has been a real problem in the States," John Lyons says.

The presence of satellite data-processing offices and telemarketing call centres in rural west Ireland suggests that the McCaffreys' plans to bring work from America to their remote part of County Fermanagh is not necessarily utopian. After my visit to KITE, in May 1995 Sheila McCaffrey gave up her full-time day job as manager of the health centre in Lisnaskea (a post she had continued to hold whilst developing the project) to take up an extended placement in the US, on an employment and training project coordinated by the US State Department. Her new role involves developing inward investment from the US, as a part of the American contribution to the peace process in the north of Ireland. The experience of KITE can, perhaps, be a model for other economically deprived areas on both sides of the border.

There is one other distinctive aspect of the KITE initiative which deserves comment. From the start of the planning process in 1988, Sheila McCaffrey was determined to ensure that child care facilities were provided as an integral part of the KITE project. She herself had recently had her first child and was aware of the problems facing other local women with children. "There were no registered day care available in the whole of Fermanagh. People in the agencies we approached said there was no need for child care, but to us it was fundamental," she says.

One of the most enjoyable parts of visiting KITE was meeting the children, who greeted their visitor with enthusiasm and posed with great smiles for my camera. There are free creche places available for up to ten children, who spend their days in a bright well-equipped nursery (there's also a quiet room attached for daytime naps). A few yards away, at the other end of the corridor, their mothers are at work in the computer suite.

KITE was exceptional. I saw very few children on my journeys for this book, but it would be too easy to draw the conclusion from this that the future of work will not be one in which the needs of children and their parents get much of a look in.

The issue deserves further investigation, if only because of the advantages which teleworking has been claimed to offer working parents – especially to women wanting to combine having a family with a career.

Where we are discussing child care, it is important to distinguish between the different types of telework. A call centre or back-office unit may be using technology innovatively to process work at a distance, but in terms of work organisation it is likely to remain a conventional workplace – not the sort of place where young children would be welcome to romp around the banks of terminals.

Home-based teleworking offers greater possibilities – in particular, the opportunity for parents to have much more opportunity to relate to their children, whilst still being able to undertake paid work.

One teleworker compared his own situation with that of his sister:

> "She is a civil servant, who leaves the house at 7.30am to beat the traffic, leaving the kids with a neighbour and getting back at 6.30pm. In contrast, I read to my children in the morning, deliver them to playgroup or child minder and by virtue of my wife working from home am able to 'mix and match' a lot more easily. It is difficult, but one hell of a lot better than the office-based alternative."[1]

Early telework writers wrote enthusiastically of the possibilities of a more 'holistic' experience, where work was once more reintegrated with home life. Sometimes the advantages were overstated: for example, it's not possible to combine *full-time* teleworking with *full-time* child care, at least where pre-school children are involved. And even home-based teleworking may involve making less than ideal arrangements: the American writer Kathleen Christensen, for example, described one woman teleworker's situation. She hires:

> "a daily babysitter from 8am to 11am, while she works in a separate upstairs office ... Although she has the benefit of strict spatial and temporal boundaries between work and family, she is not exempt from conflict. She feels torn and guilty hearing her son cry ... Often she covers her ears or puts on ear phones so as not to jump up and rush downstairs."[2]

The great divide between work and the rest of life diminishes the emotional breadth of many men's lives and offers for many women the painful choice between career development and family. It is disappointing how infrequently there is debate on just how a society might be able satisfactorily to combine the child care needs of its members with the requirements of work.

   Home-based teleworking may provide an answer. But other developing forms of telework seem set on continuing to leave children marginalised. KITE's determination to make the day-nursery an integral part of its project is particularly encouraging, therefore. It shows that this isn't inevitable – it can be done.

References

1 Private communication to the author.
2 'Impacts of Computer-Mediated Home-based Work on Women and their Familes', Kathleen E Christensen in *Office: Technology and People*, November 1987.

Journey 9

Talgarth, Powys

The telecottage movement in Britain and Ireland

A recent issue of the Telecottage Association's magazine includes a map of the British Isles, marking the location of well over a hundred telecottages. The geographical range is impressive: from Mevagissey Telecottage in Cornwall to Isles Telecroft in Shetland, East Kent Telecottage to Ness Telecottage near Stornoway, and in Ireland from the Information Technology Centre in Letterkenny, County Donegal to Comharchumann Chléire Teo on the Irish-speaking Clear Island southwest of Cork.

These local initiatives have a great deal which they *don't* share in common. They differ in how they describe themselves: some prefer the term telecentre, or electronic village hall, or teleworking centre. They differ in their legal structure: some are run as commercial businesses, some are registered charities, many occupy the middle ground as part of the community-based voluntary sector. Some are based in schools, some in libraries and village halls, others in shop premises or self-contained buildings. Telecottages differ, too, in the services they offer: IT training, printing, business services, employment provision.

But nonetheless, the British and Irish telecottages clearly constitute a movement, and a movement which has grown very quickly. A similar map produced by the Telecottage Association early in 1993 showed only 63 locations. Go back a further two or three years, and the telecottage idea was still primarily one of expectation rather than reality. A press release in 1991 spoke proudly of "six centres in operation with another known 30 projects waiting in the wings".

This history can be traced back further, to an influential conference on telecommunications and rural economic regeneration held in Cirencester in 1989 and organised by ACRE, the Association of Rural Community Councils in England. One of the speakers at the conference was Ashley Dobbs, whose career to date had spanned underwater photography, documentary film-making and property restoration and development, and who has since gone on to develop a 'televillage' at Crickhowell in Powys. (He is also currently the Telecottage Association's chairman.) Ashley Dobbs had attended a conference in Germany in late 1988 organised by the European Council for the Village and Small Town, and had come into contact with Scandinavian ideas for the development of community teleservice centres. Ashley returned to Britain to set up 'Telecottages UK', part of an early attempt to create Telecottages International, TCI.

Ashley Dobbs publicised the example of the telecottage opened in September 1985 in the remote Swedish town of Vemdalen. As he told the Cirencester conference:

> "Employment in Vemdalen from forestry and tourism was in decline and the population of the village was reducing as the younger generation went to work in the cities in southern Sweden. The Swedish authorities and telephone company provided the funding for this sophisticated telecottage with approximately £100,000 worth of computers and telecommunications facilities. Initially the villagers were invited on free courses and were allowed to 'play' with a computer so they became familiar with the equipment ... News of this successful experiment spread quickly and representatives from communities all over Scandinavia came to Vemdalen. The Nordic Association of Telecottages FILIN now represents about 50 telecottages."[1]

The person responsible for Vemdalen was Henning Albrechtsen who had retired to the area after a colourful career as an academic and author. He in turn had been influenced by plans for rural regeneration using information technology discussed in the Danish area of Lemvig in western Jutland.

However, the idea of developing remote telecentres had also surfaced elsewhere. The University of California, Davis, study on telecommuting[2] describes the work centre set up by a number of French government bodies in Marne-la-Vallee in January 1981. It was located in a residential area outside Paris and was originally envisaged as a work base for employees for 10 to 15 organisations, although it operated for only a short time. The UCD study also mentions the 'neighbourhood work centre' at Nykvarn, a small town near Stockholm which operated from 1982 to about 1985. In Britain, the Oxford-based Daily Information (still listed among the Telecottage Association's centres) claims a history back to 1975, when it first began to provide computer resources to students.

Nevertheless it was the Swedish experience at Vemdalen, as described by Ashley Dobbs and his Telecottages UK, which provided the model for later developments in Britain. Although some involved in telecottages now feel less than happy about the term's rustic overtones, at the time it carried exactly the right combination of country idyll with high-tech modernity. Journalists fell on the idea.

Indeed by 1992, when ACRE organised a second conference on telecottages, the idea was sufficiently well established for the event to feature as a storyline in BBC Radio's 'The Archers'. For a few weeks, listeners could follow plans by Archers' character Susan Carter to create a telecottage in Ambridge.

By the time of the 1992 conference, ACRE was able to share the conference organisation with a newly created body, the Telecottage Association. What had happened in the interim was that ACRE had established a two-year teleworking project, designed to develop interest both in home-based telework and in the telecottage concept, and had persuaded BT to provide £30,000 a year in funding. Alan Denbigh, who had a background in computer software, was appointed as the paid worker for this project. He himself teleworked from his home near Stroud.

Much of the credit for the development of the Telecottage Association, and of the telecottage movement more generally, rests with Alan

Denbigh, who ran a series of seminars and developed the ACRE project to a stage at the end where over 2,000 people had identified themselves as interested in the concept and who received the project's regular newsletter. By late 1992, when the ACRE project was coming to an end, there was enough support to be able to set up the Telecottage Association. Alan Denbigh moved across to become the Association's executive director. The Association itself produced a business plan which attracted further support for a two to three year period from BT, the Rural Development Commission and Apple Computers UK, with further support being offered by the Calouste Gulbenkian Foundation, the National Rural Enterprise Centre and Kay & Co Ltd.

The Association began with 400 members from ACRE's newsletter list and has now developed to the stage where it has 2,400 paid-up members, a bi-monthly magazine and a series of regional groupings, with a strong likelihood that it could continue its work even if grant-funding completely dried up. Its method of functioning is itself interesting. Alan Denbigh continues to work from home (from an office in a pine cabin in the garden), whilst the administration of the Association (including dealing with routine telephone calls) has been subcontracted out to an affiliated telecottage, the Wren Centre at Stoneleigh, Warwickshire. Other work for the magazine is outsourced to the Cork Teleworking Centre, while the Association's series of seminars are also organised remotely, for example by the Durham Dales Centre in Weardale. The Association's directors (elected at each year's AGM) regularly hold their meetings by telephone conference, using the community teleconference facilities provided to the voluntary sector by the registered charity Community Network.

The Association provides an obvious first point of contact for the telecottage movement. It works closely and collaboratively with separate national associations in Scotland, Ireland and Wales, which in each case bring together local telecottages and activists involved in teleworking initiatives for regular meetings and conferences.

Telecottages Ireland was set up in November 1993 by a number of pioneering projects, including the East Clare Telecottage in Scariff,

TeleTeach (a telecottage in the Gaeltacht area of County Donegal) and the commercially run Cork Teleworking Centre. The organisation links projects throughout the island of Ireland, and its first major event was a conference organised by KITE and held in Enniskillen in October 1994 (by luck, in the strange and hopeful time immediately after the announcement of the paramilitary ceasefire in the North). By December 1994, the association had 150 members, including 15 telecottages.

One visitor to Enniskillen was Roy Guthrie, who was involved in developing his own telecottage business in Falkirk. Roy was instrumental in convening a teleworking conference in Falkirk in March 1995, at which the Scottish Teleworking Association came into being.

Telecottages Wales/TeleFythynnod Cymru is the longest established of the three bodies, having been set up at about the same time as the Telecottage Association was being brought into being. The organisation developed after a meeting held in Aberystwyth in the summer of 1991, aided by a well-publicised visit by Henning Albrechtsen to a number of early telecottages in Wales. Telecottages Wales, which is a registered educational charity, received early grant-funding from the Welsh Development Agency, the Development Board for Rural Wales and the Calouste Gulbenkian Foundation, enabling the organisation to employ a full-time development worker, Paddy Moindrot, for about 18 months.

My visit to KITE in Kinawley had offered me one model for the work of a telecottage. But as I was to find as I travelled round the country, there are different approaches in other places. Indeed, each telecottage has its own feel, its own priorities and its own ways of generating income.

I went first to Wales, to the county of Powys. The small town of Talgarth, between Hay on Wye and Brecon, is squashed hard against the English border. The first talk of a telecottage here or in the next-door town of Bronllys took place in 1992, with both Talgarth Town Council and Bronllys Community Council supportive. Early hopes of support from the Welsh Office were dashed, however, and a bid in 1993 for European Social Fund (ESF) money from the European Commission for training was also turned down. But late in 1993, word came through that the ESF funds would after all be available, as a result of an underspend. The project hurriedly came to life.

The ESF money had to be spent by 31 March 1994. Initial plans were amended to provide for 25 local people to have 14 weeks' training in basic IT skills. But there were further delays, both in approving the revised bid and in sorting out a building. Eventually, the project got off the ground in February. "The trainees had 128 hours' training within an eight week period, working six days a week," says Amelia Jones, manager of the centre. ESF funds worth about £19,000 were matched with funding from public sources in Wales, a further £23,750. This included about £12,000 of computer equipment supplied by the Powys rural enterprise body Menter Powys.

Then, abruptly, the ESF-funded training stopped and the telecottage had to consider its future. "We decided to carry on. We feel we can make this a success, though in the meantime it's hard work. We have low wages and no funding from anyone, but lots of help from volunteers," Amelia Jones says.

In August 1994, the project moved from a portable cabin behind a hospital building in Bronllys to an old shop premises in Talgarth. The picture windows proudly advertise the presence of a 'telecentre' in the town. "People do come in to ask where the telephone is, or how much we charge for TVs, but we are beginning to get quite well known," says Amelia Jones.

Bronllys and Talgarth Telecentre has been incorporated as a company limited by guarantee, with nine directors (including four worker directors and two directors from the community). To date, it has pinned its hopes on training. The centre runs a series of one-day courses, on topics such as DTP, computer graphics, spreadsheets and keyboard skills. Courses cost between £15 to £25. The centre also runs two-hourly courses spread over 12 weeks, again on basic computer-related skills. Like the original ESF course, these are typically geared towards women returners.

The telecentre is also attempting to develop commercially orientated computer training, for which it charges about £45 per person per day. Early clients have included the local Family Health Services Authority.

Bronllys and Talgarth Telecentre is lucky in having Amelia Jones, a former IT college tutor, as its manager. She talks realistically about the need to diversify the telecottage away from training into other, perhaps more profitable, areas. The centre currently acts as a small-scale office bureau, providing photocopying (5p to 10p a sheet) and fax facilities (at BT charges, plus 50p). Staff offer a copy typing and audio typing service (£1.25 to £1.75 per page), and DTP. Recent DTP work includes posters for local pubs, a booklet of children's poetry written by a local woman and a brochure for the neighbourhood LETS (Local Exchange Trading Scheme).

The telecentre's PCs are also available for use on an hourly basis, for £4 an hour (reductions for non-commercial usage to £2 and for children to £1). A number of local children use the facilities for after-school project work and homework. More formal links with the local high school are developing only slowly.

The Talgarth centre thus is already demonstrating that it has a useful role to play in the life of its community, although it is handicapped by having to pay commercial rent for its present shop building. It is clearly still feeling its way forward, and is able to continue in large part due to the commitment of Amelia Jones and the other part-time staff and their acceptance of low wages. Amelia feels there are possible business opportunities yet to explore: a proposal to bring residential courses from London to the area, making use both of the telecentre and of local hotels and B&Bs is one idea which has been raised. The telecentre may also benefit now that an ISDN line and video-conferencing facilities have been put in.

Talgarth is typical of a number of telecottages which have begun by concentrating on the IT training side of their work, often under the incentive of European Social Fund grant-funding, and then explored ways of diversifying. But the county of Powys, which has about ten telecottages for a population of only 117,000, is a good illustration of just how diverse the telecottage movement can be. At Newtown, for example, Castell-y-dail telecottage provides a base where adults with special needs receive training in basic work skills (the centre is funded by Powys social services). At Presteigne, Crickhowell, Machynlleth and Builth Wells, the telecottages have been developed as part of a community enterprise project and are housed in secondary school premises.

Just a few miles north of Talgarth is yet another model. The CEB Telecentre at Boughrood is housed in a large wooden chalet attached to the home of Nic and Belinda Carter-Jones. Nic is a quantity surveyor and uses the building as his office for his building specification and estimation work (CEB stands for 'computer estimating bureau'). It is equipped with three PCs with CAD and DTP software, a laser printer and a colour ink jet printer.

About two years ago he arranged to open these facilities to the public, and now advertises the building as a telecentre. Menter Powys contributed £2,000 towards equipment and for building alterations, but CEB is unusual in Powys in being a privately-owned purely commercial telecottage. "People drop by with photocopying requests, or wanting to have society newsletters or membership cards printed," Nic Carter-Jones says. He estimates that, on average, about four to five people come to the centre each day, almost all previous customers. Unlike nearby Talgarth, he does not make equipment available for people to use themselves, or organise training. "It's a question of working out where the profit is. All telecottages need a specialism to succeed."

Nic Carter-Jones is in many ways a typical example of a home-based professional teleworker living in a rural area, the sort of person featured in newspaper articles on teleworking. Apart from commercial considerations, there is another advantage of opening up his office to public access. "It's a way of helping to combat isolation," he says.

References

1 'Telecottages in the United Kingdom' by Ashley Dobbs in *Teleworking and Telecottages*, report of ACRE/Royal Agricultural College Centre for Rural Studies seminar, October 1989.

2 *Telecommuting Centers and Related Concepts: A Review of Practice* by Michael N Bagley, Jill S Mannering, Patricia L Mokhtarian, University of California, Davis (Institute of Transportation Studies), March 1994.

Journey 10

Manchester

The urban context

It is easy to assume that telecottages are a purely rural phenomenon. But as a recent Telecottage Association survey found, this is not necessarily the case. In a report based on responses from about 60 centres, it concluded that about half are located in remote rural settings or small villages with most of the remaining half to be found in small towns. "A small but significant group are city-based," it added.[1]

This should not surprise. If the principle of teleworking means that jobs can be brought down the telecommunication highways to remote workers there is no reason why these workers necessarily need to be *geographically* remote. In fact, several writers have noted that home-based individual teleworkers are more often working from urban or suburban areas rather than from country areas.[2]

It is also true that inner-cities need new opportunities for employment as much as rural areas.

This was the Frontline Initiative's guiding principle, as it took shape in 1988. The project was ambitious. The idea was to create about 800 jobs by developing large teleworking centres deliberately located in commercially unattractive areas of the inner cities. A feasibility study was undertaken and the locations chosen: Leeds, Preston, Doncaster, Nottingham and East Birmingham were each to have about 146 people in post, with a smaller marketing centre for the project based in North Kensington, west London.

A report published by the National Economic Development Council (Nedc) in 1989 set out the Frontline case.[3] The plan was to recruit unemployed, inexperienced workers who would be trained to optimise their potential, rather than moulded to preconceived business needs. The idea was to "identify markets and products that match available and developing human resources, rather than resourcing to match pre-defined output requirements". The feasibility study suggested that possible services could include word processing, data input, client support services, market research, back-up and disaster recovery or in-house user support.

The Frontline Initiative was planned as a charitable trust (linked to a trading management company) which would raise at least £300,000 from the private sector, a sum which the Department of Trade and Industry agreed to match. Corporate supporters of the scheme included Alfred Marks, BP, British Rail, BT, Digital, IBM and Rank Xerox. The Trades Union Congress was also represented on the steering group.

The Frontline Initiative was grandiose enough to have developed into a spectacular success or an equally spectacular failure. In fact, it collapsed almost before it had got underway. One of the project's consultants now puts the blame on the sudden economic slump of the late 1980s – the Frontline Initiative, he says, was planned in a time of boom and had no chance of surviving the chills of recession.

But if this large-scale top-down approach proved unviable, a different idea was about to be tried in inner-city Manchester. Thanks to a generous £250,000 grant from BT's community funds and a number of smaller grants from other sources, three community organisations in the city were given the chance in 1991 to become 'electronic village halls'.

A paper prepared for Manchester City Council councillors in December 1990 explained the principle:

> "EVHs, adapted from similar rural ventures in Scandinavia, are to be located in areas of greatest need predominantly in the inner city. Some will have very specific geographical coverage for a particular community (or even a specific neighbourhood, eg a housing estate). Others will specialise in facilities for and by women, ethnic minorities, and disabled people on a city-wide basis."[4]

Community organisations were invited to tender for EVH funds, and the three successful projects were guaranteed capital equipment and two years' revenue funding. The three chosen were the Chorlton Workshop EVH (based at a training project in Chorlton, southwest of the city centre), the Greater Manchester Bangladeshi Association EVH (based in Bangladesh House in Longsight, to the southeast) and the Manchester Women's EVH (originally planned as part of the Pankhurst Centre project but eventually located in a separate building just north of the city centre).

It's necessary to put the EVH story in context. In 1989 the City Council began to develop plans for a local computer information and communications service, which became known as the Manchester Host. The idea was promoted particularly by one City Council officer, Dave Spooner, who had previously explored alternative and community-based possibilities for on-line technology whilst working in the glory days of Ken Livingstone's GLC.

The Manchester Host, a database server offering E-mail, bulletin boards, fax and telex facilities as well as access to commercial on-line database services, was launched in the spring of 1991. The capital cost of £300,000 was met from Urban Programme funds, 75 per cent paid by the Department of the Environment. The management of the Host was given to a workers' cooperative, Soft Solution Ltd.

The original Manchester Host feasibility study described at length the commercial and non-commercial uses to which the technology could be put, but said surprisingly little about the prospects for job creation through teleworking. There was clearly a reluctance to support ways of working which could be seen as exploitative: the study pointed out that home-based telework could "increase certain groups' social and career isolation and 'ghettoise' their employment opportunities". But there was also the suggestion that the development of the electronic village halls would enable 'communal teleworking' to take place, especially for women with child care responsibilities.[5]

In reality, this has failed to happen. Much of the activity in the three funded EVHs has been training based. Chorlton Workshop, for example, was previously well-established as a community-based training agency, undertaking work with local people, particularly the unemployed. The EVH grant enabled the project to survive a funding crisis and to develop its existing programme of basic computer training.

Chorlton Workshop is based in a large old church hall which has been partitioned into smaller areas. The eight PCs used for training are on trolleys, enabling them to be wheeled out for classes but locked away in large cupboards in the evenings, when the hall has other users. The training timetable typically includes an introductory ten-week computing course held for two hours once a week, and a more intensive programme of courses over 18 weeks leading to the RSA CLAIT (computer literacy and information technology) qualification. A free creche for children aged between six months and five years is normally available whilst the courses are running, and each course has a substantial waiting list.

As well as the timetabled courses, the Workshop also runs a computer drop-in session for women on Monday afternoons and a similar open access session for anyone on Wednesday afternoons. These free sessions include the opportunity to explore the Internet, accessed through the Manchester Host.

"In theory, the original idea was that we would be an urban telecottage. In practice, we have put much more emphasis on working with the unemployed. We try to target ourselves specifically to people who wouldn't go to college, students who don't already have further education qualifications. We prioritise black people and people with pre-school children," says Andy Robinson, one of the centre's workers. The Workshop also runs basic maths and English courses, as well as craft-based sessions in sewing, machine knitting and silk-screen printing.

Like many other community-based voluntary sector projects, Chorlton Workshop has to live in a state of permanent uncertainty over the next year's grant funding. Currently its annual income of about £75,000 is patched together from a variety of sources, including the Further Education Funding Council (routed via the WEA) and a number of charitable trusts. The project recently failed in an attempt to obtain European Social Fund training money, but is likely to benefit from Manchester's European Regional Development Fund (ERDF) bid.

Although Chorlton Workshop advertises that its computer, fax and E-mail facilities are available for hire at low cost to local organisations and small businesses, in practice the take-up has been very limited. In 1993 only £310 came into the centre in income from this service.

The Bangladesh House EVH is also primarily a training venture offering RSA accredited courses. The Greater Manchester Bangladeshi Association developed in the 1970s from an initial base at a mosque and now has a large building offering sports and social facilities, and welfare advice. Before becoming an EVH, the Association had previously developed its training work and was for a time a Manpower Services Agency centre. Computer training remains a core activity, now funded through the local Training and Enterprise Council (typically, about a third of the trainees are from the Bangladeshi community, the remainder coming from other ethnic backgrounds).

The Bangladesh House EVH has also been associated with the Manchester Asian Trading Information Network (Matin) project, which has aimed to develop computerised information links between Asian-owned businesses in the city, and also between them and businesses and institutions in the Indian sub-continent. The Matin project workers organised a conference on the use of telematics in international trade, held in Bangladesh in 1993.

The third of the original funded EVHs, the Women's Electronic Village Hall, also offers computer training facilities, with child care expenses paid for those participating. The Women's EVH offers drop-in access times twice a week. According to its introductory leaflet, "We aim to meet the varied needs of all women; as well as having a network of PCs and Apple Macs, we have a Braille printer, Minicom, Speech Synthesiser and fully accessible premises ... Any woman or women's group can come along and use the resources at the centre, for example to produce their own newsletter, design leaflets or just to drop in for a chat and cup of tea."[6]

Since the launch of the Host computer and the start of the EVH initiative, Manchester has gone on to promote itself as an 'Information City', and is currently coordinating the Telecities grouping of city authorities within the European Union interested in developing telematics services. A successful recent bid for European Regional Development Fund (ERDF) money will enable it to upgrade the Host facilities, whilst a series of substantial further bids will, if approved, allow the funding of up to eight more EVHs. A number of other EVH projects, including a Disabled Peoples' EVH, have already been established in the city by a variety of community groups.

Manchester's initiatives have been watched, and copied, by other local authorities. Kirklees Metropolitan Council in west Yorkshire now has an exact parallel set-up (its Kirklees Host computer is also managed by Soft Solution co-operative). As part of the project, a Disabled People's Electronic Village Hall has been set up in a day centre in Dewsbury.

Whilst it is interesting to see local authorities promoting telematic services in their areas, there is something of a contradiction here: why install a locally-based host computer when the whole point of the technology is that it knows no geographical boundaries? (Wakefield council, which is developing a Wakefield Host, has avoided taking the hardware option and is creating a 'virtual' host on the Kirklees machine.)

Clearly, we are still at a very early stage of exploring how communities can make use of the possibilities of the information age. There is, however, a clear underlying issue which individual initiatives like these are trying to address: how in our information age of the future can we ensure that all citizens have access to that information? How democratic will the Information Society turn out to be?

At the level of national and international strategy this issue is at least already acknowledged. The US administration's Agenda for Action on the National Information Infrastructure talks of the need to avoid "a division of our people among telecommunications or information 'haves' and 'have-nots'".[7] The Bangemann report from the European Union echoed the same phrasing, commenting that "The main risk lies in the creation of a two-tier society of haves and have-nots, in which only a part of the population has access to the new technology, is comfortable using it and can fully enjoy its benefits."[8]

In Britain, the Labour Party talks of ensuring that schools, hospitals, libraries and community centres are given automatic rights of access on to the evolving broadband information highways. But quite how communities will make use of this access is far from clear. Today's telecottages and electronic village halls are valuable in identifying what is, and isn't, going to work.

References

1 *Teleworker*, February/March 1995.
2 See, for example, *Review of Telework in Britain: Implications for Public Policy*. Prepared for the Parliamentary Office of Science and Technology by Andrew Gillespie, Ranald Richardson and James Cornford, Centre for Urban and Regional Development Studies, University of Newcastle upon Tyne, February 1995, page 30/31.
3 *Working by Wire: Teleworking and the Frontline Initiative*, National Economic Development Council, 1989.
4 *The Manchester Host and Technology Programmes*, progress report from Manchester City Council Chief Executive's Department, December 1990.
5 *The Manchester Host Computer Feasibility Study, Final Report May 1990* by Bernard Leach, Clare Girbash, Steve Walker, Shaun Fensom. Centre for Employment Research, Manchester Polytechnic.
6 *Women in Computing* leaflet. See also *A Women's Computer Centre at the Pankhurst Centre*, undated.
7 *The National Information Infrastructure: Agenda for Action*, 1993.
8 *Europe and the Global Information Society, Recommendations to the European Council* (the 'Bangemann report'), June 1994.

Journey 11

Maiden Newton, Dorset

What future for the telecottages?

As with a number of other telecottages, the initial funding has just run out at Boon. Boon – the name turns out to stand, slightly mysteriously, for Business On Open Network – occupies part of the old station building in the village of Maiden Newton just north of Dorchester. Every now and then, a diesel unit stops noisily at the platform outside: the trains still come this way, on the rural cross-country line from Bristol down to Weymouth, passing quiet stations like Bruton, Yetminster and Chetnole on the way. Everyone knows it's not the most secure of railway services, but the community is doing what it can to ensure that the trains keep running.

Drew Llewellyn, Boon's manager, is just as determined to make sure his project survives. Boon has been grant-funded from its start-up in May 1992 by three bodies, the Rural Development Commission, Dorset County Council and the local district council. However, the grants were arranged on a decreasing year-on-year basis. For 1994-5, for example, support was cut to £18,000, down from the previous year's £30,000 figure. "And from April 1995, we're without funding," Drew Llewellyn says.

The many real-life telecottages which sprang into life about the time of that fictional storyline in 'The Archers' in 1992 are now two or three years further on. In many cases, initial funding was justified as necessary to cover start-up costs. However there was frequently an assumption, not always explicit, that a time would come when telecottages would have found their commercial feet, and would be able to continue without further support. Already some funding agencies are beginning to ask what they have got for their money.

When I visited the Mere telecottage in Wiltshire early in 1995, for example, the manager there was working under notice of redundancy, with the funding due to be cut off at the end of March. Mere telecottage, based in a former staff rest-room in the village's public library, had opened in April 1991 to considerable national media interest: TV cameras from both Meridian and HTV had come calling. The Community Council for Wiltshire, the sponsoring organisation, subsequently went on to support two further telecottages in the county, in Crudwell near Malmesbury and Codford near Warminster. At Codford in particular the telecottage quickly made its mark on local life, and after a period when it was based in a back room of a local pub it found a more permanent home in a side-room in the newly built village hall.

However late in 1994 a reorganisation of CCW's employment projects into a separate commercial subsidiary left all three telecottages vulnerable. Trevor Bailey, CCW's assistant director, was quoted as saying that the future "will depend upon a reappraisal of the telecottages' local role and, above all, an input of skills and facilities to achieve wide commercial work on a thoroughly realistic scale". Another CCW manager, Carol Drew, added that "the lead time needed to establish the telecottages was longer than anticipated ... CCW had hoped that additional income would come from large contracts but these did not come to fruition after long negotiations."[1]

In the event the March 31st deadline came with no decision taken. Mere telecottage continued on a voluntary-run basis, whilst Codford and Crudwell were closed. At time of writing it looks as though Codford may be able to re-open as an independent locally-run centre, whilst the other two telecottages may have a future as part of a commercial concern.

The experience of the Wiltshire telecottages is interesting, if only because the Community Council for Wiltshire seemed to do many things right. In July 1993 a marketing development officer was appointed, responsible for promoting the business potential of the three centres. For a time, it looked as though a major contract was on its way from

Derwent Publications Ltd. Derwent, one of the market leaders in scientific and patents information, was interested in using teleworkers to abstract and classify newly filed patents.

But though the Derwent work did not develop as planned, some outsourcing work did come through. At Codford in particular, local women undertook data processing work for a housing survey for the MoD on Salisbury Plain. "Until September 1994, we had four teleworkers at a time, two full-time and the rest part-time, and all women. The majority had children at school, and it was the only chance they had to work," says Janet Nuth, manager at Codford. The telework pay was an hourly rate of £4.

Janet Nuth believes that telecottages could still band together, perhaps on a county-wide basis, to undertake outsourcing work for large companies. "But telecottages would have to get their act together. Each county would need to have good management structures, to ensure quality and confidentiality. You need a marketing manager – it would be impossible for me to go out and make the contacts."

Ironically, Codford telecottage was probably close to breaking even when CCW called its future into question. As well as organising the teleworking contract, the centre had also been used for regular training courses, mainly through the New Opportunities for Women scheme. It also offered access to the village's only photocopier and public fax machine, whilst Janet Nuth took bookings for the village hall.

Moira telecottage in north-west Leicestershire has also been searching for the key to commercial viability, though in a very different situation from the telecottages of Wiltshire. Moira is an urban village, in the old south Derbyshire/north-west Leicestershire coalfields. This is an area which may have a green future (it is in the heart of the area designated for the proposed new National Forest) but at the moment there is all too much evidence of the past, including a great deal of derelict land.

The telecottage is in a single-storey building which was once a branch library, next door to the large house where Moira Replan, a local charitable organisation which has been working hard for the economic regeneration of the area for eight years, is based. Moira Replan developed the telecottage about two years ago, initially with plans for it to be a separate trading venture. "Unlike other telecottages who do a lot of computer training, we envisaged it as a commercial operation offering services to local businesses," says Graham Knight of Moira Replan.

The telecottage has provided the focus for the creation of a business club locally, and a number of seminars on aspects of running a small business have been held in the centre's comfortable meeting room. "Members of the business club use the telecottage if they want to send a fax or get word-processing done and we provide a telephone answering service for about two or three people. One person who is developing a water purification system and is on the brink of successful expansion has met business clients here rather than at home," says Graham Knight.

But it has become clear that the telecottage will not be able to survive as a purely commercial venture on this basis, and the project is being re-absorbed in the parent Replan body. "I have a problem with the idea that telecottages provide an access place to IT equipment. The technology is now so available to anyone, and small businesses are increasingly getting their own computer equipment," Graham Knight says.

The survey of telecottages carried out in the *Teleworker* magazine in February/March 1995 reported that one in seven said that they were currently profit-making, one-third were making a loss, whilst 'a half … claimed to be breaking even'. The report went on, "Overall, half of the centres are continuing to be subsidised in some way."

Clearly, quite a lot of public money has been channelled over the past few years into the telecottage movement. The report on teleworking carried out by the University of Newcastle upon Tyne CURDS researchers looked into the question of funding in more detail:

> "The telecottage has emerged as the most popular mechanism for development agencies and local authorities wishing to develop information and communications related initiatives. The link between telecottages and local development strategies is most sharply shown by the number of telecottages which received start-up funding. In all some 81per cent of the telecottages in the [1993] sample [of 42

telecottages] received start-up funding. Development agencies were the most common funders, with local authorities and 'other' funders (mainly BT's Community Programme) coming next ... More than half the telecottages claimed to be no longer receiving ongoing funding, but almost half of these were undertaking work for a public agency and this might be seen as a surrogate form of public support. Ongoing funding again comes mainly from development agencies, local authorities and the European Community."[2]

There is no reason why telecottages should necessarily feel defensive about receiving grant-support for their activities. After all, purely commercial ventures are also eligible in some circumstances for public assistance. (We have seen already how Hoskyns' operation in Forres and the American telemarketing organisations coaxed into Ireland have received substantial help from public funds.)

But clearly, it's useful to work out what it is that telecottages are doing which justifies giving them support. Different telecottages find work in different ways, but their activities can perhaps be put into four categories:
  – Training
  – Office bureau facilities
  – Community development
  – Providing telework/employment brokerage.

Many telecottages have begun by concentrating on the IT training side of their work. This was, as we have seen, how KITE in Kinawley began. It is how Talgarth and the Manchester EVHs, in their very different settings, serve their local communities. It has been important at Codford. Indeed, the University of Newcastle upon Tyne CURDS survey reported that 69 per cent of telecottages (29 out of 42) listed training as one of their main activities.

Clearly this is potentially valuable work, both for the individuals who receive training and, more generally, for the opportunity provided to increase an understanding of IT within the population as a whole. In several cases, training is undertaken for the (relatively basic) RSA CLAIT series of courses. However, Moorlands telecottage in Warslow near Buxton has been instrumental in developing a formal National Vocational Qualification for teleworkers, combining elements of IT, business administration and finance and self-management skills. The telework NVQ was launched in 1994, and the syllabus is being followed in a number of telecottages.

From the telecottage's point of view training can be a precarious base for longer-term planning given the vagaries of funding support, especially from the European Social Fund. Telecottages can suffer as local authority adult education budgets are cut, and may also discover that they are in competition with local colleges of education for IT training. There is the further risk that the pool of local people, especially women, interested in basic computer training will eventually dry up.

Community-based training does not by itself usually generate very much income. Charges are potentially much higher if commercial IT training can be undertaken for business clients. However, to develop this market demands a business-like approach which may clash with telecottages' commitments to their community activities (managers on a spreadsheet familiarisation course are unlikely to want to share a training room with local schoolchildren undertaking their homework, for example). Furthermore, telecottages contemplating commercial computer training require staff with up-to-date IT experience, suitably state-of-the-art hardware and software and an adequate training space. (Of course, ideally trainees on community courses should have a right to expect these, too.)

My 'office bureau facilities' category for telecottages includes many things. Moira telecottage gives some idea of the range in its list of the services it offers: 'telephone answering, mail handling, photocopying, fax service, word processing, data processing, accounts/bookkeeping, computer hire, room hire'. Other telecottages undertake DTP graphics and printing work, sell computer accessories and stationery, and provide access facilities to on-line databases and services (though the evidence suggests that this sort of service is only rarely requested). A number of telecottages act as agents for Kays mail order service, with access to

Kays' computerised stock lists.

In larger centres of population, many of these bureau services will be available commercially. But this is not the case everywhere. The Arkleton Trust, in its 1993 report on the six Community Teleservice Centres (CTCs) established in the Scottish Highlands and Islands, argues why public funding may be legitimate:

> "There is a demand for telecoms based, DTP and office related services from small and micro enterprises, from a rich variety [of] voluntary organisations and from individuals, even in islands with small communities (Unst 1,000, Hoy 500). Fulfilling this demand through a collective facility (such as a telecottage) is more cost-effective than each purchasing their own equipment ...
>
> "In essence there is a 'market failure' to provide essential services in such small and isolated communities which will naturally tend to under-provision, and hence disadvantage, local businesses and organisations ... If public policy ... both recognises the need and agrees that it should be met, then the bodies involved should act jointly to provide at least some of the core funding required to support CTCs in providing such basic services."[3]

This links to my third category, what I have called 'community development'. This is harder to describe, mainly because much of the work is informal. It clearly includes the sort of work with schoolchildren being undertaken in Talgarth. It also covers the small business advisory role undertaken at Moira telecottage. I saw it demonstrated on a visit to Scariff, East Clare, in the focus which the telecottage there provides to other economic and community regeneration projects in the area.

But I also mean something more nebulous: the sort of unquantifiable low-level support which a telecottage can provide to a community, and to individuals within that community. This can perhaps best be seen reflected in the idea that having a telecottage is generally a 'good thing'. (Other communal facilities, including a village shop or pub, can fulfil a similar role.) Of course, whether this function merits public money, and if so how much, is open to debate.

It is in Kington, Herefordshire, that the possibilities for community enrichment using information and communications technology is being put most obviously to the test. Kington was successful in 1993 in a competition run by Apple Computers, BT, the DTI and the Rural Development Commission and modelled on a similar experiment run by Apple Computers in the small town of Jacksonville, Oregon. The community group in Kington which emerged to develop the project described in its 97-page bid how computer use would be developed in all aspects of the town's life, including local business, social activity and schooling. What Kington won as a result was about £250,000 of equipment; on the back of the win, the project has also been able to attract substantial revenue funding.

With so much money and public interest riding on the success of the project, Kington was perhaps being set up for almost inevitable failure. In fact, not all the early high hopes have been realised but nevertheless much good work has been undertaken. Less than two years on, it's too early to attempt a complete assessment of the project.

And so, finally, to what some people might consider the chief function of a telecottage, its role as a remote centre where teleworking can take place. We have already seen how KITE is attempting to develop this function. Other telecottages, including the Kington telecentre and also the Warwickshire Rural Enterprise Network (Wren) telecottage at Stoneleigh, have also worked hard to find suitable work.

But – even though remote working is clearly an important and growing phenomenon – the role of telecottages in attracting this work has been problematic. The University of Newcastle upon Tyne CURDS report offered a fairly gloomy assessment of the difficulties:

> "Whilst possession of marketable skills may be a necessary condition if a telecottage is to win contracts from remote businesses, it is not a sufficient condition. A number of problems remain, not least of which include how the telecottage identifies its potential customers and how it gains access to these businesses, in order to make its business case. In the unlikely event that the telecottage is able to overcome these

hurdles it is now in a competitive environment and must continually improve its efficiency to retain the business it has won."[4]

The report goes on to draw attention to the experience at the Antur Tanat Cain project based at Llangedwyn Mill, southwest of Oswestry. In 1991, Paddy Moindrot, who was involved in developing what had begun in 1979 as a community-based job creation agency, could quite fairly describe Antur Tanat Cain as 'a major telework project'. For a time, up to 20 local people in this remote part of mid-Wales were undertaking text inputting and data processing work.

"We had been building the vocational training we were doing, and were looking around for real work," Paddy Moindrot says. Fortuitously, a report in a local paper of the organisation's work happened to be seen by an ICL consultant living locally. Through this contact, Antur Tanat Cain won a number of sizeable contracts from the company. Some of the work was undertaken by trainees at the Llangedwyn Mill base and some subcontracted out to home-based teleworkers, several of them former trainees. "Every Wednesday the data inputters brought back their week's work and collected more to type, and this 'changeover day' fulfilled a need for social interaction."[5]

Unfortunately, a variety of factors including the onset of the recession meant that the ICL contracts dried up, and teleworking has now more or less ceased at Llangedwyn. The University of Newcastle upon Tyne report assesses the experience as follows:

> "The Antur case ... demonstrates that even when telecottages are successful in overcoming the hurdles involved in winning remote work, considerable pressures, which will be familiar to small businesses in competitive markets, remain. For example, significant capital investment may be required to keep pace with technological change, but this investment is risky as customers may seek downward variations in price or may withdraw the work if a more competitive supplier can be found."[6]

One of the strengths of the telecottage movement is that each is normally autonomous, rooted in its neighbourhood, and with strong local accountability and support. But this can also be a weakness: individual telecottages are small undertakings, relatively inexperienced in marketing themselves to the outside world.

Wiltshire's attempt to use a county-wide marketing officer to find work for its telecottages has been adopted also in Powys, where the telecottages have use of a professionally produced publicity brochure into which they can insert their own material. The Telecottage Association has worked to increase the business skills of telecottage staff with a series of one-day seminars, and has recently encouraged telecottages to consider applying for the ISO9000 quality standard.

One telework possibility could be for telecottages to undertake outsourced work for public authorities. The Arkleton Trust report on the Community Teleservice Centres in the Highlands and Islands suggested that funding bodies might consider this as a form of indirect support:

> "It may be more useful to provide project work to CTCs as a partial or complete alternative to revenue grants. The latter tend to encourage unrealistic overheads ... whilst the former would have provided useful experience in project work. Such things as entering records on databases, undertaking local skills surveys, preparing databases of local businesses and self-employed people and the like could not only provide important local information but would also help CTCs to establish a track record from the start."[7]

Ultimately, perhaps, the success of each telecottage depends in large measure on the individuals who work there, and on how entrepreneurial they are in seeking out development opportunities.

Drew Llewellyn at Boon in Maiden Newton is confident that his project will survive the ending of grant support. As outside in the rain a few passengers wait for the next train south to Dorchester, inside Drew is enthusiastically reviewing for me the various strands in Boon's work. There is the computer maintenance service, cornily but effectively named Mouse to Mouse Resuscitation. There is the training work, undertaken on a one-to-one basis at £50 for each three-hour session. There is the data management work for Dorset County Council, pulling together information on business opportunities in the area. There is Country Work Computing, a project sponsored by the Post Office and the RDC, which has enabled Boon to lend laptops and modems to local small businesses at modest rates of hire (£50 a month).

And there is also the work Boon has been undertaking in joint marketing for locally based teleworkers. Drew Llewellyn describes how one Japanese linguist has developed a translation service, aided by on-line distribution provided from the telecentre. The project has raised the profile of teleworking in the Dorset area, and publicised the economic, environmental and social benefits, he argues.

Drew Llewellyn's energy and enthusiasm is infectious. "I'm really excited about computers and their possibilities," he says. And it is hard not to believe him when he says that Boon can continue. "We'll be OK," he says.

References

1 'Wiltshire network seeks new focus', in *Teleworker*, April/May 1995.
2 *A Review of Telework in Britain: Implications for Public Policy*. Prepared for the Parliamentary Office of Science and Technology by Andrew Gillespie, Ranald Richardson and James Cornford, Centre for Urban and Regional Development Studies, University of Newcastle upon Tyne, February 1995.
3 *Final report on the evaluation of Community Teleservice Centres in the Highlands And Islands* by John Bryden, Stuart Black, Frank Rennie, for The Arkleton Trust (Research) Ltd, August 1993.
4 See note 2 above.
5 'Managing a major telework project' by Paddy Moindrot in *Teleworking – Real Business Benefits*, proceedings of British Computer Society seminar, 9 October 1991.
6 See note 2 above.
7 See note 3 above.

Journey 12

Brussels

The European Commission and telework

If telework technology has the potential to abolish geography, it's perhaps worth remembering that distance isn't just a geographical term. Distance is also a social and cultural construct.

Geographically speaking Brussels is not really very far away, even from the farthest corners of the British Isles. But for many people the inverted-commas 'Brussels' where 'Europe' has its home can seem impossibly distant and elusive.

As far as telework is concerned, however, the location of this second 'Brussels' can be identified quite precisely. Take the metro from the city centre out towards the southeastern suburbs, get off at Beaulieu station and stroll down the hill. Inside the modern office block on your left are the offices of staff from Directorate-General 13 (DG XIII) who over the past few years have seen it as their job to stimulate the development of teleworking in Europe. They have been active: talking at conferences, commissioning consultants, grant-funding research projects and overseeing the publication of a bewildering mass of material. Telework may not yet be a household word in each of the eleven official European Union languages, but at least now it must be in the dictionaries.

Here is how the subject is introduced in one of their brochures:

"Telework may be part of your future working life. The telecommunications and computer revolutions have now opened up a wide range of new, more flexible ways of working, with at least part of the time outside a traditional office ...These new ways of working are at the centre of the European Commission's policy for growth, business competitiveness and new employment."[1]

Anyone who is attempting an account of teleworking in the European context clearly has to take note of what the European Commission has been doing. But there are different ways in which this role can be assessed.

For example, it is possible to follow what might loosely be called the British tabloid approach to 'Brussels', portraying the Commission as a bloated bureaucracy spending its time on worthless work. This assessment would question the value of the Commission's involvement in telework. It could, for example, point to the piles of publications produced and question whether anyone is reading them. It could challenge the Commission's apparent role in encouraging the emergence of a caste of telework consultants, trotting from one conference to another.

It could focus on the apparent impenetrability of Commission life: the complex structures, the endless acronyms for programmes and projects. It could comment on the Commission's perceived delight in imposing words such as 'additionality' and 'concertation' on a long-suffering English language.

Or it could criticise the Commission for its role as sugar daddy, distributing largesse to anyone able to get a grant application containing the word 'telematics' in at the right time to the right address.

As with caricatures, there are elements of truth in this sort of account. But the view from inside Avenue de Beaulieu would, I suspect, look rather different. And the case for the defence would no doubt point out that – compared certainly to the mandarin culture of the British Civil Service – the Commission's staff are by and large approachable and helpful, that the structures are not so hard to understand for anyone who takes the trouble and that – given the problems of running a supranational organisation where national interests often collide – actually the Commission can operate surprisingly efficiently.

But above all, a defence of the telework initiatives emanating from

Brussels would be arguing that the Commission is taking a necessary strategic overview of one important element in the development of jobs and employment for the whole continent. Someone has to take the lead in planning for the future of work.

There are two key documents which have emerged from within the structures of the European Union, which help set the overall context for this activity. At the end of 1993, the White Paper *Growth, Competitiveness and Employment* was released by the Commission. This lengthy report, usually described as the Delors White Paper, was an attempted overview of the prospects for the European economy, and was particularly concerned with tackling the problems of unemployment. The report promoted the concept of the 'information society', a choice of wording which may not resonate particularly easily in English but which has now become an important term within the European Commission and the EU generally.

A recent Commission document explained the central concept: "The general preference in the United States until recently was for the term 'information highways', implying a more limited, technology-based appreciation of what is happening. By contrast, 'information society' reflects European concerns with the broader social and organisational changes which will flow from the information and communications revolution."[2]

According to the Delors White Paper, the promotion of telework was one necessary step in order to promote the increased use of information technologies within Europe.

The White Paper was quickly followed, in June 1994, by the production of a report entitled *Europe and the Global Information Society*, known as the Bangemann Report after Martin Bangemann, the European Commissioner who chaired the committee which produced it. This was a grouping of nineteen senior industrialists, including the chairmen or chief executives of many of the most important telecoms and IT companies in Europe, known (with no attempt at unbecoming modesty) as the 'high-level group on the information society'.

The Bangemann report was presented to the summit of EU leaders held in Corfu in June 1994. It stresses the importance of ensuring that existing state-owned telecoms companies in EU member states are opened up to market forces ('liberalised'). The private sector, according to Bangemann, is to play the main role in driving forward the information society initiative. But it also identifies telework as the first of ten applications of the technology (others include distance learning, university networks and public administration networks) which it believes can act as demonstrations of the potential of the information society.

Teleworking, the report claims, means "more jobs, new jobs, for a mobile society". It goes on:

> "Companies (both large and SMEs [small and medium-sized enterprises]) and public administrations will benefit from productivity gains, increased flexibility, cost savings. For the general public, pollution levels, traffic congestion and energy consumption will be reduced. For employees, more flexible working arrangements will be particularly beneficial for all those tied to the home, and for people in remote locations the narrowing of distances will help cohesion."[3]

It then sets the following target for the European Union member states [at that stage, 12 strong]: "The aim is for 2 per cent of white collar workers to be teleworkers by 1996; 10 million teleworking jobs by the year 2000".

Without a standard definition of teleworking, it's probably not unduly cynical to suggest that the European Commission will almost certainly be able to claim it has successfully reached these targets. However telework is not an occupation in itself, but simply a way of undertaking work. The Bangemann report talked of 'more jobs, new jobs'. Certainly the development of technology may create new types of jobs and new ways of performing them; it's not at all clear that this will also mean 'more jobs'.

Before we go further into the details, however, it's sensible to get an overview of all the European Commission's areas of activity which could affect teleworking. As we shall see, DG XIII is not the only directorate-general with an interest in the issue. (The Commission is structured into

24 DGs, performing a similar role to that of ministries in the British Civil Service; conventionally, DGs are described using roman numerals.)

There are three main areas to consider.

The first is regional development. The European Union makes large amounts of money available for regional development through the European Regional Development Fund (ERDF), one of the EU's so-called structural funds designed to remedy economic disparities between different parts of the Union. The money set aside for the structural funds has been growing and is now very substantial: 141 billion ECU (or about £110 bn) for the years 1994-1999.

There are various eligibility rules for regional development aid: 'Objective 1' regions are those areas considered to have most catching-up to do with other parts of the EU (for example, the whole of Ireland is an Objective 1 area, as is the Scottish Highlands and Islands). Declining industrial areas may have 'Objective 2' status whilst rural areas suffering from serious problems of decline can be designated 'Objective 5b' areas, making them also eligible for ERDF support.

The bulk of ERDF funding is distributed not from the Commission but through national or regional governments. In England the DTI and Department of the Environment together control and oversee the distribution of the country's share of this money, working through a network of Integrated Regional Offices.

The Commission has a greater say in how a small percentage (currently 9 per cent) of the structural funds budget is spent, the part set aside for 'Community Initiatives'. These are EU-wide programmes designed to resolve problems being experienced across member-state boundaries. The Commission also controls a remaining 1 per cent sliver of the structural funds budget, which has been set aside for innovative pilot projects.

In the past, some money from the 'Community Initiatives' share of the budget has been channelled into programmes such as STAR (Special Telecommunications Action for Regional Development) and TELEMATICS, both designed to promote advanced telecoms services in disadvantaged regions. These have now been replaced by, among others, the SME programme (focusing on the business needs of small and medium-sized enterprises), the Urban Community Initiative and the rural economic development programme LEADER II.

Regional development is the responsibility of the Commission's Directorate-General 16 (DG XVI). DG XVI is currently collaborating with DG XIII and six regions of the EU (including the north west of England) in a pilot 'Regional Information Society Initiative'. The six regions have identified themselves as prepared to 'promote universal access to the opportunities and advantages of the information society with a view to generating new employment opportunities'.[4] DG XVI is keen to extend this initiative to other regions within the EU.

Employment and social affairs is the responsibility of a different Directorate-General, DG V. DG V administers another structural fund, the European Social Fund. Whilst this can be used – like the ERDF – to support Objectives 1, 2 and 5b, it can also be used for Objectives 3 (combatting long-term unemployment and improving employment chances for the young) and 4 (adapting the workforce to industrial change).[5]

As with ERDF funding, national and regional governments rather than the European Commission decide how the bulk of ESF funding is to be spent. In Britain, applications are normally routed through a variety of regional or sectoral organisations including the Training and Enterprise Councils.

Again as with the ERDF, the European Commission (in this case DG V) has a greater role in deciding how the 'Community Initiatives' part of the budget will be used. For the years 1994-1999, DG V is coordinating the Adapt Community Initiative, primarily designed to promote training, and three linked strands in an Employment and Human Resources Community Initiative, catering for the training and employment needs of women (the Now programme), disabled and disadvantaged groups (Horizon) and young people (Youthstart). We have already seen how important the ESF (especially New Opportunities for Women/NOW funding) has been in supporting the computer training work carried out by many telecottages. Whilst the Community Initiatives programmes are developed centrally by the Commission, distribution of the funds is coordinated through central government bodies in each member state.

DG V has an interest in the various issues of employment protection, health and safety and employment legislation raised by new forms of working such as teleworking. Indeed teleworking was one of the issues investigated in 1993 by a working group which studied the prevalence of homeworking (mainly traditional forms of home-based work) in EU countries for the Commission.

The authors of this report reported generally:

> "Pay and conditions for homeworkers are generally inferior to those for other workers. Even where hourly rates are relatively good, their employment is insecure … For most homeworkers, their flexibility means long hours of work at low pay, with few of the rights taken for granted by the majority of the workers in Europe."

They then considered the anticipated growth in home-based teleworking, and added:

> "The concern is that if the main growth in teleworking is in the lower grade, telehomeworking end of the scale, this will mainly be used as a form of cost-cutting to develop a more flexible workforce, with similar results to telehomeworkers as for traditional homeworkers … While the extent of this low-paid sector is likely to happen invisibly, telework for higher paid professionals is the form of employment which attracts the publicity …"[6]

After the publication of the Delors White Paper, DG V returned to the issue of home-based telework, commissioning a review of the social, employment and regulatory issues involved from Ursula Huws. Her report included a number of recommendations for EU policy and for future research, and concluded:

> "Whilst it offers enormous opportunities for creating employment and enhancing prosperity into the 21st Century, the widespread introduction of teleworking is also capable of bringing with it a

number of undesirable side-effects. Most of these side-effects can, however, be avoided, if the new technologies are introduced in a regulated manner, with resources directed towards minimising the social damage to vulnerable groups within the EU."[7]

The EU's social and employment policy is a politically controversial subject, at least with the present British government. DG V could however choose to flex its legislative muscle in this area. There will be particular pressure to resolve legislative anomalies between member states if teleworking across national borders begins to develop widely in the EU.

This brings us back to DG XIII, and to the third main area where European Commission actions may have an impact on teleworking.

As I visited British and Irish telecottages early in the Spring of 1995 there was increasing evidence of hurried preparations underway to meet a March deadline for proposals for EU funding for research projects. Partners were being sought; draft proposals were being discussed by E-mail or in closed discussion groups on CompuServe's Telework Europa forum; final drafts were being typed up, ready for submission. In at least one case, the arrangements included hand-delivery of the proposal direct to Avenue de Beaulieu on the day of the deadline itself.

The telecottages were applying to participate in the Telematics Applications Programme, a small part of the Commission's overall support for research and technology development. This has been a long-established area for EU funding: the Third Framework Programme ran from 1990 to 1994, and has now been replaced by the Fourth Framework Programme, which is due to run until 1998.

The Telematics Applications programme, administered by DG XIII, has been allocated a total of 843 million ECU (about £680 million), about seven per cent of the Commission's total budget for the Fourth Framework Programme. Telematics is defined as 'the application of information and communications technologies and services, usually in direct combination', and the programme is structured to encourage research projects into uses in, for example, central and local government, transport, libraries and health care. Whilst teleworking could fit in a number of these areas, it has its own place in the programme, in a category called 'urban and rural areas'.

According to the Commission, possible research tasks under the programme include:
- 'develop, test and validate teleworking applications to support the growth and maintenance of existing rural-based communities';
- 'develop, test and validate telematics systems to support teleworkers who are constrained by personal or other circumstances (eg parents with young children, people with caring responsibilities, etc)';
- 'develop, test and validate teleworking schemes to help re-integrate the unemployed';
- 'develop, test and validate teleworking and teleservices in the context of self-help' initiatives for the economically deprived or the socially excluded'.[8]

Most telecottages have chosen not to be involved in EU-funded research projects or have not had the resources to join in. As with other EU-funded programmes, projects have to be transnational, involving organisations in more than one member state. Some British and Irish telecottages, however, have already had experience of successfully applying for EU-funded research. In particular, a number were involved in the 'Telework Stimulation Programme', developed and co-ordinated by DG XIII and announced in 1993. Under this programme about 33 separate research projects were funded, most of them running over eighteen months until the summer of 1995.

For example, the Wren telecottage in Stoneleigh through its parent body the Royal Agricultural Society of England was the lead partner in 'Offnet', an 18-month project researching the management of neighbourhood telecentres. Offnet included Austrian and east German partners and also drew support from the Telecottage Association and Telecottages Wales. The Cork Teleworking Centre participated in 'Regiodesk', a Belgian-led project aimed at disseminating information on teleworking to practitioners. The Manchester Women's Electronic Village Hall was a partner in 'SBN' a research venture which looked at the possibility for electronic data interchange between small businesses.

The Brussels acronym phenomenon is much in evidence here, with other projects in the Telework Stimulation programme having names like TELDET (Telework Developments and Trends), EVONET (European Virtual Office Network), TELEURBA (Telework and Urban and Interurban Traffic Decongestion), RITE (Regional Infrastructure for Teleworking) and ATTICA (Analysis of Constraints to Transborder Telework in the European Community). Anyone anxious to find out the results of these projects will find the information available from DG XIII.[9]

The intention within the Commission's DG XIII is for telework-linked projects funded under the Telematics Applications Programme to build on the momentum of the 1994-5 Telework Stimulation Programme.

But what, in practice, does it all mean? A few more research projects, a few more conferences, a few more reports to be filed at the end? Inside Avenue de Beaulieu, Peter Johnston of DG XIII admits candidly that not all the research projects produce much of value, though he talks of the value nonetheless of finding 'diamonds among the mud' and says that things can be learned even from the failures. His own involvement in the subject goes back a long way, as one of the speakers at the 1989 Cirencester conference which as we have seen kick-started the telecottage movement in Britain.

There have been a lot more conferences since then, and many more papers delivered. But the message tends to remain the same: telework is an important option in the restructuring of European industry. "Over 50 per cent of employment in Europe now involves information management," Peter Johnston told a conference audience in January 1995. "Competitive advantage now lies in the use of telecommunications and information technologies to support much more flexible and decentralised business organisations … Telework is now an attractive option in most service industries."[10]

References

1 *Telework Stimulation*, European Commission DG XIII-B (ref CD8594591ENC).
2 *Introduction to the Information Society: The European Way*, booklet from

Information Society Project Office, 1995.

3 *Europe and the Global Information Society, Recommendations to the European Council* (the 'Bangemann report'), June 1994.

4 *Regional Information Society Initiative, Memorandum of Understanding*, 28 November 1994.

5 For those who may be wondering, Objective 5a is concerned with adapting agriculture and modernising the fishing industry. Two separate, smaller, structural funds have been set up to meet this objective.

6 *Homeworking in the EC*, report of the ad hoc working group, rapporteur Jane Tate, European Commission, Document reference V/7173/93EN.

7 *Teleworking, Follow-up to the White Paper, Report to the European Commission's Employment Task Force (Directorate General V)* by Ursula Huws, September 1994, Ref V/1697/94EN.

8 *Telematics Applications Programme (1994-1998)*. Work programme and annex, 15 December 1994.

9 For a general account of the programme, see: *Actions for stimulation of transborder telework and research cooperation in Europe/Telework 1995*, European Commission DB XIII-B [1995].

10 *Working on the Infobahn – a European View: Telework Development in context of The White Paper on Growth, Competitiveness and Employment*, paper by Peter Johnston to 'Working on the Infobahn' conference, Manchester, January 1995.

See also: *Technical Publications related to Advanced Communications Technologies And Services, Information Security, Telework*, vol III, prepared in 1994 by the A-Staff of DGXIII-B.

Journey 13

Strathdon, Aberdeenshire

Plans for a teleworking future

So who's teleworking now? Liz Burn and Amanda Stewart-Richardson are, at least some of the time. So are the other eighteen members of the community business which together they have established in Strathdon, up on the edge of the Grampians a few miles north of Balmoral.

It's still early days in Strathdon, but there is much enthusiasm here for teleworking. The local Upper Donside Community Trust got things moving by organising a conference on the subject, held in the autumn of 1994. During the event a list was passed around, which anyone interested in taking the idea further was invited to sign. And so Strathdon Telematic Services (Grampian) Ltd, a company limited by guarantee, came into being. The 20 members each contributed £20 to join and now meet about every six weeks, to discuss how things are developing. Liz, Amanda and two other local women comprise the steering group and are legally the company's directors.

And the work has already started arriving. Elizabeth Duncan of EBD Associates, the Aberdeen-based business which takes subcontracted work from Crossaig, is in turn further subcontracting some of this to the women of Strathdon. Other women are engaged in data entry work for the publisher Longmans, again via EBD Associates. The Community Trust itself has offered work producing a newsletter and undertaking market research work in the locality. There is still not enough work for everyone to work all the time, but the members of Strathdon Telematic Services feel they have made a promising start. Pay is on a piecework basis, but for anyone working fairly efficiently can work out at about £4 to £5 an hour.

In a small neighbourhood like Strathdon, there is a strong community spirit to carry forward a venture like this. Though most people work from home, Strathdon Telematic Services currently has a base in a converted studio next door to Liz Burn's home. It was here that Liz and Amanda met me, to outline their future plans. This is a women's venture (only one of the 20 members is a man). According to Liz, whose own husband works away in the oil industry, many of the members are wives of local farmers, most with children at school. "We were all here, not doing any work. But we found that a lot of people had PCs at home: in fact, fifteen people have 486s," she says. "People are grateful now to have the work, and to have a few extra pounds in their pockets."

The Community Trust remains involved and there is talk now of creating a telecottage in the village. Staff from Grampian Regional Council are also offering advice. The necessary energy and commitment is there, but – as the experience of KITE and some of the English and Welsh telecottages shows – the on going task of creating employment through teleworking is not necessarily unproblematic. It's still early days.

It seems appropriate to end these journeys of mine at Strathdon, with a visit to a community group which is just beginning to explore the possibilities which telework may provide. In a moment, I want to return for a final time to some of the questions I outlined in the introduction: what can we expect from telework? Is this what we want from work?

But first there is the journey home.

My interest in telework began some years ago, from direct experience. Like many writers, I work from an office in my home. Since my writing these days is done with the aid of a computer and a fax machine and a smart little modem with red flashing lights, I think that I meet the criteria to qualify as a teleworker.

In the global information society, my PC and desk could be – almost – anywhere. It happens to be in west Yorkshire, in a town in one of the Pennine valleys where the first Industrial Revolution got under way two hundred years or more ago. Technology transformed the traditional home-based manufacturing of the area, first in spinning and then later on in weaving.

The population was gradually drawn down from the hilltop farms and villages into the valley bottoms, and into the mills. Not everyone wanted the change. A few miles over the hills to the south, the hand-croppers physically tried to resist the moves to mechanisation by destroying the machines which were replacing their highly-valued labour. The croppers called on a mythical Ned Ludd to lead them to victory, but of course they lost. Rather unfairly (since after all they were only trying to save their jobs), their name is used by history to describe anyone who fails to appreciate and embrace technological change.

Visit my town today, 200 years on from this seismic social transformation, and what would you see? A few mills are still working, but many are now dedicated to the tourist trade. The canal, which when it was first pushed through the hills opened up the whole the area for trade, is now used for leisure boating. Service industries have now clearly replaced manufacturing in economic importance.

Not everything about the economic life of this part of northern England is immediately visible, however. A few years back, Mercury negotiated with the canal company to dig up the towpath. A couple of feet down can be found the fibre optic cable they laid then, a key part of the company's trunk network. Under the feet of the tourists, gigabyte upon gigabyte of information now passes backwards and forwards between Manchester, the Yorkshire cities and the world.

Here, in other words, is the economic infrastructure for the work of the 21st century already in place. Scratch the picture-postcard view and underneath lies the future of work.

Conclusion

Telework can mean many things.

It can mean taking employees out of the workplace and putting them back in their homes. It can mean transferring back-office work to remote data processing centres or outsourcing it altogether.

It can refer to the growing practice of developing specialist call centres, automating the process of using the telephone in business transactions with customers. It can be the sometimes elusive goal for telecottages, struggling to find a secure source of income to replace initial grant-funding.

And it can, indeed, mean taking advantage of technology to leave the rat-race behind and recreate your office, sweet office, in a rose-covered cottage in the country.

Telework, under the definition I outlined in the introduction, has two characteristics: the use of information and communication technologies to practise remote working of some kind. In other words, telework is not an occupation, but a method of working. It is developing as technologies develop, offering new opportunities for distance-independent work. But telework is not primarily a technology issue.

It is one element of a general restructuring process which businesses have been engaged in, and which has been gathering speed over the past fifteen years. We have become used to hearing the new terms for this process gradually slipping into business-speak: downsizing, rightsizing, business process re-engineering, outsourcing, and so many more. But the essence of this process of restructuring has been the business imperative to maintain profit levels, and one way to do this has been by increasing the flexibility of the workforce.

Flexibility is telework's other name, as I hope this book has demonstrated. BT at Southampton, for example, has developed more flexible staffing rosters through using home-based staff. Crossaig's use of employees based at home on piece rates allows it to recruit from a wider labour pool and to cope efficiently with fluctuating work-loads. Telecottages such as KITE offer companies access to a flexible pool of labour.

Companies who make use of telework are likely to find that they can push more of their business risks further down the chain. For example, responsibilities towards staff are picked up instead by telecottages or outsourcing agencies, or in the case of self-employed freelance teleworkers are passed entirely to the individual worker. Even where teleworkers remain employees some of the risk element can be transferred, if for example staff are prepared to adjust their working hours to the flow of work. (This does not mean, of course, that I am suggesting that companies using teleworking are consciously taking part in some sort of deliberate process of exploitation: they are simply searching for ways to maintain their competitive position.)

There can thus be commercial advantages for companies in making use of teleworking. There are potential advantages, too, for individuals. There are many people who find the teleworking experience satisfying and fulfilling. More flexibility at work is a valuable gain for individuals as well as companies.

In addition to benefits for companies and individuals, there are advantages claimed for society as a whole from teleworking. These can potentially include "a reduction in urban traffic congestion, energy conservation, air quality improvement, revitalization of urban areas, and economic growth for rural areas"[1]. The importance of telecommuting, to use the American term, has been reinforced in California and elsewhere in the US, where legislation has been introduced to control the number of commuter journeys made by car.

The experiences of individuals who are teleworking and of the community-based telecottage movement are important. In terms of overall economic importance, however, the development of remote call centres and back-office sites is likely to have more of an influence on people's lives.

After several weeks on the road journeying to some of the most beautiful parts of the British Isles (and once there searching out the industrial estates), I want to comment particularly on two aspects of what I found: the first is that the telejobs appear to be going primarily to women and the second is an observation on the rates of pay on offer.

It has been striking how, again and again, the telework locations I have visited have been predominantly places of work for women. Both at the large remote satellite offices like Cigna's at Loughrea and the community-based telecottages, it has been women who have made up the bulk of the workforce. (Indeed, in one or two cases, only the management has been male.)

This might suggest that, if the future is in teleworking, the future for the male gender is not looking very bright. But there are a number of explanations for this phenomenon. Clearly, much of the routine office-based secretarial and administrative work in our society has traditionally been undertaken by women, so it is hardly surprising to find women predominantly filling these posts in the new back-office sites. The technology may have changed, but there are many similarities between a remote data-processing centre and, say, an old-fashioned telephone exchange or a typing pool.

But I would argue beyond this that teleworking is a modern manifestation of a more fundamental, and long-established, phenomenon in society. For years, many women have made up a parallel, informal, labour force running alongside what could be called the 'official' labour force. The latter – the pool of people who are, primarily, full-time (or, if unemployed, would-be full-time) workers and who are undertaking readily recognised 'real' jobs – gets most attention from economists, statisticians and social observers.

Whilst women have increasingly joined men in this world of jobs and careers, not many men have chosen to cross over to join women in the informal world of the parallel labour market, however. This pool of extra labour provides valuable flexibility for the economy: when business is booming, more people can be drawn into employment. But during slumps this labour force tends to slip quietly away out of sight, and find other things to do. Many women, especially those with family commitments, are familiar with the experience of piecing together different sources of income. The emphasis here is on 'work' rather than 'jobs'. It may be that the work is paid child-minding for neighbours, casual shop work, cleaning work, or the traditional types of low-status homeworking such as sewing. Or it may be, especially for those people who have professional education and experience, that the work comes from such things as freelance editing, or creative craftwork, or translation, or shifts as locums or holiday relief staff.

We have been told by commentators like Charles Handy that the days are passing when people can expect a job for life, accompanied by the classic linear career graph rising steadily upwards through the years. But many women in this parallel labour force have long had a great deal of experience of what Handy pronounces as the future trend, putting together a 'work portfolio' of different jobs and work opportunities.[2]

Many of the possibilities which have been created by the telework initiatives I have described in this book, whether in the commercial sector or via community-based ventures like telecottages, fall firmly within this category of work. The work is flexible, and often not full-time; the hours can frequently be tailored around other commitments; the work can be undertaken in the home or not far away in the locality; the work comes without assumptions of much career progression. So it is perhaps not surprising to find that it is mainly women doing it.

So what about the wage-levels available to teleworkers?

This is always going to be a sensitive subject, and I do not want to be simplistic. Telework does not in itself equal worker exploitation (as we saw in chapter 4 the trade unions themselves in general do not argue this). Since teleworking is a way of working rather than a type of work, the money earned by teleworkers will obviously vary according to their skills, their experience and the sort of work they are undertaking – a civil engineer will earn more than someone undertaking typing work, for example, whether they are teleworking or not. The case of Crossaig shows that working from home does not necessarily mean poor rates of pay: Rosemary Rattney estimated her hourly rate as up to £17.50 an hour, for instance.

The question rather is whether there is anything inherent in the telework situation which would mean that, say, a teleworking civil engineer would end up with less than an office-based person doing the same work. This area needs more empirical research, possibly using a larger pool of teleworkers than we currently have available. But any changes in the employment status of teleworkers (especially moves from employee to self-employed status) may have major implications on their remuneration. (These changes could, of course, be upwards as well as downwards.)

In the longer term, moves towards a more fragmented and atomised workforce might suggest a weakening of the ability of workers to maintain their collective bargaining power and therefore also their wage rates.

To the extent that telework is seen as a female phenomenon, pay rates could suffer from the historical fact that (the Equal Pay Act notwithstanding) women are, as a body, paid less than their male counterparts in society.

It is when we focus in from a general consideration of teleworking to the specific cases of back-office/call centre teleworking that a concern about the relationship between telework and pay levels can begin to seem more immediately relevant.

Pay is, of course, relative. Again and again on these journeys when I enquired about the money on offer, telework companies told me they were paying over the odds compared with other employers locally and I am happy to believe them. But of course, £8,000 to £10,000 a year for someone in a rural area where the cost of living is low might seem acceptable to an extent which is unimaginable to somebody living, say, in central London. However, this is not necessarily the point.

Pay is relative, but if telework renders geographical distance irrelevant is there any longer anything to prevent jobs seeping away from the big cities and the high-wage areas? Like water flowing from the top of a hill to the valley bottom, will the jobs also find their own level where wage rates are lowest? If this is true, although the development of teleworking could be hopeful for some living in economically remote areas, it could be a very worrying prospect for many others.

In fact, we can assume that a number of factors will restrict the extent to which this process takes place. The labour market is by no means a perfect market and all sorts of factors distort its operation.

The location of work is never likely to be something which market forces alone are allowed to decide: if nothing else, politicians will see to that. It is also not clear whether the technology which makes telework possible will in itself be sufficient to turn us all into distance workers.

Nevertheless, these are issues of some importance. Perhaps the most important of all is that telework is oblivious of national boundaries. In other words there is not necessarily any guarantee that, as the jobs move to find their level, they won't in the process migrate to other parts of the world, where labour is even cheaper. Some low-value work, such as repetitive data processing, is already being outsourced to countries in the Indian subcontinent or the Far East.

It is not just low-value telework which may go overseas. A number of airline companies, for example, have begun to transfer aspects of their operation to lower-wage areas. British Airways has had a small centre in New Delhi since 1990, charged with the task of resolving inaccurate or incomplete entries on the company's computerised booking system. More ambitiously, Swissair employs 370 staff in an office in Bombay to handle all its ticket accounting and computer entry queries.

There is a developing computer software industry in India servicing clients in the West. Here, for example, is what S K Pandit has written about one venture:

> "At BAeHAL Software's offices in Bangalore, in southern India, a computer programmer keys in a change to a programme he is writing for a UK client. The computer he is using, via a satellite link, is at the

client's site in Bristol. Because it is morning in Bangalore but still night in England, there are few users and the computer responds faster to him than it would to a user on the client's site, during the working day there. By the time the client comes to work, the changes will have been completed and tested."[3]

I believe that increasingly the international context will be essential to a proper understanding of teleworking: a world economy where many of the services we need can, both in theory and increasingly in practice, be provided irrespective of national boundaries.

We are back to what I tried to suggest in my first journey of this book: the idea that Whalley, Lancs could as easily be West Bengal.

Some people will welcome these developments as a way of helping to transfer wealth to the underdeveloped countries of the 'South'. Others will want to defend their own interests. The Bangemann report from the 'high-level group on the information society' was worried, for example, that western Europe's economic dominance was under challenge: "Competitive suppliers of networks and services from outside Europe are increasingly active in our markets", it reported, stressing the need for urgency.[4] "Preparing Europeans for the advent of the information society is a priority task. Education, training and promotion will necessarily play a central role."

There are always contradictory pressures in any process of change. Whilst the technological changes which are happening at the moment are in many ways immensely exciting, there are dangers as well as opportunities.

But it would be inappropriate to end on too gloomy a note. Bangemann consulted his high-level group. I have tried in this book also to listen to the 'low-level groups' – the ventures and initiatives which are concerned at a practical level in identifying and creating the jobs of the future. As at Strathdon, there is a lot of energetic interest in ways that we can take advantage of technology, in the process making sure that the changes that come do so on our own terms.

Individuals can benefit enormously from the work opportunities which the technology is bringing – for example, if they find work which was previously unavailable to them, or if the flexibility of this work allows them to tailor it more easily to their family life and other commitments. In general the teleworkers I met during these journeys were happy with their working situation, were aware of the snags but were keen to emphasise the advantages.

Telework has plenty of potential to change our working lives, and our home lives, for the better. Our task is to try to make sure that the potential is realised – and this is going to be a social, rather than a technological, challenge. Not everything planned will work out, and not every high hope will be realised. But what encourages me is that people in their communities are engaging in the issues and pondering ways in which the changes that are coming can be harnessed for good. That surely is, in itself, cause for hope.

References

1 *Telecommuting Centers and Related Concepts: A Review of Practice* by Michael N Bagley, Jill S Mannering, Patricia L Mokhtarian, University of California, Davis (Institute of Transportation Studies), March 1994.
2 See *The Age of Unreason* Charles Handy, Business Books, 1989 and *The Empty Raincoat* Charles Handy, Hutchinson, 1994.
3 'Wired to the rest of the world', S.K. 'Juggy' Pandit, *Financial Times*, 10 January 1995 (Winner of the *Financial Times*' 1994 David Thomas Prize).
4 *Europe and the Global Information Society, Recommendations to the European Council* (the 'Bangemann report'), June 1994.

Bibliography

ACRE (Action with Communities in Rural England): *Teleworking and Telecottages*, papers presented at the seminar organised jointly by ACRE and CRS, 17 October 1989, 1990.

Paul S Adler (ed): *Technology and the Future of Work*, Oxford University Press, 1992.

Michael N Bagley, Jill S Mannering, Patricia L Mokhtarian: *Telecommuting Centers and Related Concepts: A Review of Practice,* Institute of Transportation Studies, University of California, Davis, March 1994. [ftp://ftp.ucdavis.edu, directory 'pub', file Tcenter.exe]

Andrew Bibby: *Home is Where the Office is, A Guide to Teleworking from Home*, Hodder Headline, 1991.

British Computer Society Data Comms Specialist Group, British Computer Society Office Automation Specialist Group, IEE Professional Group: *Teleworking – Real Business Benefits*, proceedings of a seminar, 9 October 1991.

F E K Britton: *Rethinking Work, An Exploratory Investigation of New Concepts of Work in a Knowledge Society: the telework option reviewed*, RACE 1994, EcoPlan International/European Commission DG XIII, n.d.

Mike Brocklehurst: 'Homeworking and the New Technology – the Reality and the Rhetoric', *Personnel Review*, vol 18, no 2, 1989.

Mike Brocklehurst: 'Combining a Career with Childcare – is New

Technology Homeworking the Way Forward?' in *Women in Management Review*, vol 4, no 4, 1989.

John Bryden, Stuart Black, Frank Rennie [the Arkleton Trust (Research) Ltd]: *Final Report on the Evaluation of Community Teleservice Centres in the Highlands and Islands*, August 1993.

BT: *Teleworking, BT's Inverness experience* [booklet], BT, 1994.

Steven Burch: *Teleworking, a strategic guide for management*, Kogan Page, 1991.

Kathleen E Christensen: 'Impacts of computer-mediated home-based work on women and their families', in *Office: Technology and People*, November 1987.

Colin and Susan Coulson-Thomas: *Implementing a Telecommuting Programme*, Adaptation Ltd, 1990.

Europe and the Global Information Society, Recommendations to the European Council (the 'Bangemann report'), June 1994.

European Commission: *Actions for Stimulation of transborder telework and research cooperation in Europe/Telework 1995*. European Commission DG XIII-B, 1995.

European Commission: *Technical Publications related to Advanced Communications Technologies and Services, Information Society, Telework*, vol III. Prepared by A staff of DG XIII-B, 1994.

European Commission: *Telematics Applications Programme (1994-1998), Work Programme*, DG XIII, 15 December 1994.

European Commission: *Introduction to the Information Society: the European Way*, Information Society Project Office, February 1995.

European Commission: *Legal, Organisational and Management Issues* in *Telework, New Ways to Work in the Virtual European Company* [reports of COBRA, PRACTICE, ATTICA projects], DG XIII n.d.

ExperTeam, TeleCom and IDATE: *European Telecommunications Handbook for Teleworkers, a study for the Commission of the European Union*, October 1994.

Tom Forester: 'The Myth of the Electronic Cottage', in *Futures*, June 1988.

Andrew Gillespie, Ranald Richardson: *Advanced Communications and Regional Development: The Highlands and Islands of Scotland*. Report undertaken as part of the ACCORDE Project, Centre for Urban and Regional Development Studies, University of Newcastle upon Tyne, August 1994.

Andrew Gillespie, Ranald Richardson and James Cornford: *Review of Telework in Britain: Implications for Public Policy*. Prepared for the Parliamentary Office of Science and Technology, Centre for Urban and Regional Development Studies, University of Newcastle upon Tyne, February 1995.

Gil Gordon: *Managing Teleworking* [booklet], BT, February 1994.

Mike Gray, Noel Hodson and Gil Gordon: *Teleworking Explained*, John Wiley and Sons, 1993.

Leslie Haddon, Roger Silverstone: *Teleworking in the 1990s – A view from the home*, University of Sussex, SPRU CICT Report series no 10, August 1993.

Noel Hodson: *The Economics of Teleworking* [booklet], BT n.d.

Ursula Huws: *The New Homeworkers, New Technology and the changing location of White-collar work*, Low Pay Unit, 1984.

Ursula Huws, Werner B Korte, Simon Robinson: *Telework, Towards the Elusive Office*, John Wiley and Sons, 1990.

Ursula Huws: *Teleworking in Britain*. A report to the Employment Department, research series no 18, October 1993.

Ursula Huws: *Teleworking (Follow up to the White Paper)*. Report to the European Commission's Employment Task Force (DG V), September 1994.

Ursula Huws: *Home Truths, Key results from a national survey of homeworkers*, National Group on Homeworking, 1994.

Ursula Huws: *A Manager's Guide to Teleworking*, Employment Department Group, 1995.

International Labour Office: *Conditions of Work Digest*, vol 9, 1/1990. Telework, ILO, Geneva.

Phillip Judkin, David West, John Drew: *Networking in Organisations: the Rank Xerox experiment*, Gower, 1985.

Francis Kinsman: *The Telecommuters*, John Wiley and Sons, 1987.

Mandy Lavery and Alison Templeton: *Flexible Working with Information Technology: the business opportunity*, Ovum Ltd, 1993.

Leeds Trade Union and Community Resource and Information Centre: *New Technology and Women's Employment, case studies from West Yorkshire*, December 1982.

M H Lyons: *A Study of the Environmental Impact of Teleworking* [booklet], BT, December 1990.

Horace Mitchell, Eric Trodd, Brameur Ltd: *DTI Teleworking Study* 1992-3. Final report, September 1993.

Horace Mitchell, Eric Trodd, Brameur Ltd: *An Introductory Study of Telework Based Transport-Telecommunications Substitution*, 1993-1994, September 1994.

National Economic Development Council: *Working by Wire: Teleworking and the Frontline Initiative*, 1989.

Jack M Nilles: *Making Telecommuting Happen: A Guide for Telemanagers and Telecommuters*, Van Nostrand Reinhold, 1994.

Reagan Mays Ramsower: *Telecommuting: The Organisational and Behavioral Effects of Working from Home*, Ann Arbor, UMI Research Press, 1985.

Alastair Reid: *Teleworking, A Guide to Good Practice*, NCC Blackwell, 1994.

Seán Ó Siochrú: *Advanced Communications for Cohesion and Regional Development*, ACCORDE:T1015 Final report, February 1995.

Smart Valley Telecommuting Guide, version 1, n.d.

Solon consultants (John Myers, Valerie Bennett, Beverley Darbyshire,

Elizabeth Davenport, Ann Leeming): *Working at a Distance*, Solon, 1992.

John and Celia Stanworth: *Telework: the Human Resource Implications*, IPM, 1991.

Jane Tate (rapporteur): *Homeworking in the EC.* Report of the ad hoc working group, European Commission DG V. n.d.

Telecottage Association: *Fact Sheets* [loose leaf folder].

Telework '94, New Ways to Work. Proceedings of the European Assembly on Teleworking and New Ways of Working, Berlin Nov 34 1994.

TeleWork '94, First European Assembly on 'New Ways to Work', Berlin Nov 34 1994, Briefing book

Alvin Toffler: *The Third Wave*, Collins, 1980.

David Tucknutt: *A Study of Homeworking Environments* [booklet], BT, April 1992.

Andrew Wilson: *Teleworking: flexibility for a few*, Institute of Manpower Studies, 1991.

John Withnell: *Corporate Teleworking, The Competitive Advantage for the Future* [booklet], BT, 1991.

Videos

Telecottages in Australia

Teleworking: BT's Inverness experiment (BT)

On-line resources

A selection of Internet and other sites with telework related material:

World Wide Web sites (home pages):

http://www.gilgordon.com [Telecommuting, teleworking and alternative offices web site, run by Gil Gordon and David Peterson]

http://www.icbl.hw.ac.uk/bill/telework [Information, esp on training, located at Heriot-Watt University, Edinburgh]

http://www.svi.org [Smart Valley initiative, California]

http://www.ispo.cec.be [European Commission Information Society Project Office]

http://www.igd.fhg.de/wise/ [EC WISE Information Board; includes telework material]

Discussion lists:

telework:

telework@mailbase.ac.uk [listowner is David Barry; subscribe by E-mail to teleworkrequest@mailbase.ac.uk]

information society:

ispo@www.ispo.cec.be [EC Information Society Project Office discussion list; subscribe with 'subscribe ispo' message + E-mail address to ispo-request@www.ispo.cec.be]

CompuServe:

Telework Europa forum: access with command GO TWEURO

Working from Home forum: access with command GO WORK

Index

ABI/Inform 58
ACRE 72-74
Albrechtsen, Henning 72, 75
Alfred Marks 80
Antur Tanat Cain 94
Apple Computers 74, 93
Archers, The 73, 86
Arkleton Trust 92, 95
Automated Call Distribution 21, 51, 53

Bangemann Report 84, 99-100, 117
Bangladesh 83
Bangladesh House EVH 81, 83
Banking 52
Barclaycard 60
BECTU (trade union) 36
Best Western Hotels 49
Boon telecottage 86, 95-96
BP 80
British Airways 116
British Rail 80
Bronllys and Talgarth telecentre 75-78, 90, 92
BT (British Telecom) 1,2,8,10, 20-25, 29, 34, 41, 45, 52, 66, 73-74, 80, 90, 93, 112

Bull 36

California Western States Life Insurance Co 33-34
Call centres 3, 5, 20-25, 48-56, 111, 113, 115
Careers and telework 17-18, 23-24, 35, 113-114
Care lines 52, 55
CD-ROM 58
CEB Telecentre 78
Charity fundraising 52-53
Children 13, 17, 30, 65, 68-70, 82, 105
Chorlton Workshop 81-83
Cigna 67, 113
Codford telecottage 87-88, 90
Community Network 74
Community Teleservice Centres (Scotland) 41, 44, 92, 95
Companies House on-line 7-8
CompuServe 57, 60-61, 104
Computer Telephony Integration 51, 55
Co-operative Bank 52
Copyright 61
Cork Teleworking Centre 74-75, 105

CPS 32, 36
Crickhowell televillage 72
Crossaig Ltd 28-32, 58, 108, 112, 115
Crudwell telecottage 87

Databases, on-line 7, 28-29, 81
Data Protection Act 17
Dell 49, 52
Delors White Paper 99, 103
Denbigh, Alan 73-74
Department of Employment 9,11, 25-26, 34
Department of the Environment 81, 101
Department of Trade & Industry 3, 60, 61-62, 80, 93, 101
Derwent Publications Ltd 88
Digital 36, 80
Direct Line 52
Disabled people 80, 84, 102
Disabled Peoples EVH 84

East Clare telecottage 74, 92
EBD Associates 32, 108
Electronic mail (E-mail) 23, 35, 36, 57, 60, 81
Electronic village halls 80-84, 105, and see telecentres
Empirica 8
Employees as teleworkers 3, 9-10, 17, 20-25, 26-27, 31-36, 112, 115
European Commission 4,5,8, 78, 97-106
European Regional Development Fund 82, 84, 101-102
European Social Fund 64, 75-77, 82, 91, 102-103
European Union 34, 43, 58, 83, 90
FI Group 33, 36

Financial Times 8, 61
First Direct 52
Flexible working 22, 24, 111-114
Forres 38-40, 42-46, 90
Fourth Framework Programme 104-105
France 9, 73
Frontline Initiative 79-80
FT Profile 58

Gateway 2000 49, 52-54
Global-Res International Ltd 48-49, 51-56
Guardian, The 13

Handy, Charles 46, 114
Health and safety 17, 21, 35-36, 103
Highlands and Islands Development Board 40-42
Highlands and Islands Enterprise 40-42
Highlands and Islands (Telecommunications) Initiative 41-43
Home, working from 1-3,8,9,12-15, 20-25, 78, 103-4
Homeworking, National Group on 16
Homeworking (traditional) 16, 103
Hoskyns 38-40, 42-43, 44-46, 90
Huws, Ursula 9-11, 25, 103

IBM 80
ICL 32, 36, 94
India 46, 116-117
Industrial Development Agency (Ireland) 50, 54-55, 66
Information society 58, 84, 99-100, 102, 117
Instant Search 6-8

Insurance 17, 52, 66-68
Intellectual property rights 61
Internationalisation of work 7, 46, 48-56, 116-118
International Labour Office 25
Internet 36, 58-62, 82
Inverness (BT pilot) 24-25, 34
Ireland 3,4, 48-51, 53-56, 63-68, 74-75, 101
Irish Times 53
ISDN (Integrated Services Digital Network) 21, 22, 29, 30, 41-42, 66, 77

Kay and Co 74, 91-92
Kington, Herefordshire 93
Kirklees Metropolitan Council 84
KITE telecottage 17, 63-66,89-90 68, 70, 75, 90, 93, 109, 112

Labour Party (UK) 59, 84-85
Liberalisation of telecoms 43, 100
Local authorities 38-40, 80-84, 95
Lochgilphead 31, 41
Lombard North Central 36
Luddites 110

Management of teleworkers 4, 22-24, 26-27, 30, 34, 44-46, 53-54
Manchester 80-84
Manchester Host 81
Marketing for telecottages 95
Market research 52
Mercury 36
Mere telecottage 87
Mitchell, Horace 9, 60-61
Moira telecottage 88-89
Moorlands telecottage 91
MSF (trade union) 35-36

National Association of Teleworkers 15
National Information Infrastructure (USA) 58, 84
National Rural Enterprise Centre 74
National Union of Journalists 36
New Opportunities for Women (NOW) 64-65, 88, 102
Nilles, Jack 2,4
NVQ in telework 91

Oliver, Chris 13-14, 17
Optical character recognition 29
Outsourcing 3, 17, 33, 38-40, 44-46, 52, 88, 111-112
OwnBase 12-15

Philippines 46
Planning permission 17

Quality standards 95

Radisson Hotels International 49
Rank Xerox 32, 36, 80
Reed Elsevier 29
RSA 82, 83, 90
Rural development 1-2,10-11, 43-44, 94-95, 102, 105
Rural Development Commission 74, 86, 93, 96

Scotland 29, 38-43, 75, 92, 101
Scottish Development Agency 29
Scottish Teleworking Association 75
Self-employed teleworkers 3, 15, 17, 32-34, 115
Semler, Ricardo 45
Sheraton Hotels 49
STAR 101
Strathdon Telematic Services 108-109, 117

Structural funds - see European Regional Development Fund, European, Social Fund
Swissair 116

Talgarth telecentre - see Bronllys and Talgarth
Taxation 17, 32, 34
Telecentres 3,4, 15, 41, 62, 63-66, 68-70, 71-78, 80-84, 86-96, 104-6, 109
Telecommuting - see Telework
Teleconferencing 74
Telecottage Association 15, 71-74, 79, 95
Telecottages - see telecentres
Telecottages International 72
Telecottages Ireland 74-75
Telecottages Wales 75
Telemarketing 3, 50-56
Telematics Applications Programme 104-106
Telesales 3, 20-25, 50-56
Teleservice: see Telesales, Telemarketing
Teletrade 60-61
Telework:
 advantages and disadvantages to companies 22-23, 25-27, 112-113
 advantages and disadvantages to individuals 16-19, 112-113
 and business restructuring 4, 33, 111-112
 and careers 17-18, 23-24, 35, 113-114
 and families 13, 18
 and internationalisation of work 7, 46, 48-56, 116-118
 and management 4, 22-24, 26-27, 30, 34, 44-46, 53-54
 and travel 16, 26, 112
 and types of occupation 10, 12
 definitions 2-3, 111
 numbers teleworking 8-10
Teleworker (magazine) 15, 89
Telework Stimulation Programme 105-106
Toffler, Alvin 2,4
Trade unions 34-36, 114
Trades Union Congress 80
Training 64, 76-77, 81-83, 88, 90-91

Unison (trade union) 36
Universal service provision 43-44

Vemdalen, Sweden 72-73
Videoconferencing 77
Videophones 23
Voice mail 51

USA 25, 33-34, 50, 55, 60-61, 66-68

Wage levels 16, 28, 35, 40, 50, 54-55, 67, 103, 114-116
Whalley, Lancs 6-8, 117
Women and telework 18-19, 24, 43, 82, 109, 113-115
Women's Electronic Village Hall 83, 105
World Wide Web 36, 59-62
Wren telecottage 74, 93, 105

Young people 102